The Complete
Chicken Cookbook

THE COMPLETE
CHICKEN COOKBOOK

Edited by

JANET SWARBRICK

CHARTWELL
BOOKS, INC.

A QUINTET BOOK

Published by Chartwell Books
A Division of Book Sales, Inc.
PO Box 7100
Edison, New Jersey 08818-7100

This edition produced for sale
in the U.S.A., its territories
and dependencies only.

ISBN 0-7858-0392-0

This book was designed and produced by
Quintet Publishing Limited
6 Blundell Street
London N7 9BH

The material in this book previously appeared in
Barbecue Cooking by Roger Hicks, *Cajun Cooking* by Marjie Lambert,
Caribbean Cooking by Devinia Sookia,
The Chicken Cookbook by Wendy Veale,
The Complete Rice Cookbook by Myra Street, *Creole Cooking* by Sue Mullin,
The Fresh Pasta Cookbook by Bridget Jones,
Lebanese Cooking by Susan Ward, *Mexican Cooking* by Roger Hicks,
Meze Cooking by Sarah Maxwell,
New Jewish Cooking by Elizabeth Wolf Cohen,
Nuevo Cubano Cooking by Sue Mullin,
Recipes from a Polish Kitchen by Bridget Jones,
Russian Regional Recipes by Susan Ward, *Salsa Cooking* by Marjie Lambert,
Southern Cooking by Marjie Lambert, *Spanish Cooking* by Pepita Aris,
Stir Fry Cooking by Bridget Jones, *Thai Cooking* by Kurt Kahrs
and *Vietnamese Cooking* by Paulette Do Van.

Creative Director: Richard Dewing
Designer: James Lawrence
Editor: Janet Swarbrick
Illustration: Greta Fenton

Typeset in Great Britain by
Central Southern Typesetters, Eastbourne
Manufactured in Singapore by Bright Arts Pte Ltd
Printed in China by Leefung-Asco Printers Ltd

Contents

Introduction

A S LONG AGO AS 3000 BC, a small Asian jungle fowl became domesticated. This was the beginning of a source of food which, through the ages, has become one of the most popular and plentiful foods of the international diet.

Due to its versatility, popularity and availability, chicken now represents many of the world's national and traditional dishes. An added bonus is that chicken answers the requirements of today's healthy eating guidelines: low in cholesterol, but high in protein and vitamins. It provides nourishing meals and is economical.

In *The Complete Chicken Cookbook* there are a number of new and exciting recipes: combinations of chicken with a wide variety of fresh, wholesome ingredients; the blending of light sauces; the minimum amount of fat and the infusion of delicate herbs and robust spices. Combined with the gentlest and most beneficial methods of cooking, the results are a delicious and nutritious contribution to a healthy diet.

Henry IV of France declared "I want there to be no peasant in my kingdom so poor that he cannot have a chicken in his pot every Sunday" – hence the famous "poulet au pot". Included here are some of the more traditional chicken dishes – from home and abroad. Ingredients are often slightly amended in favor of healthier alternatives, but the unique flavor and characteristics of the dish are still there to be savored.

The recipes in *The Complete Chicken Cookbook* have been prepared for the health conscious cook, providing mouthwatering and nutritious dishes for every occasion.

METHODS OF COOKING CHICKEN

There are four main methods of cooking whole and portioned chickens and several alternative and less familiar or obvious cooking methods.

ROASTING

Traditionalists still find great comfort in, and enjoy the ritual of, a roast dinner. It is home cooking at its best and, more often than not, is an occasion shared with a number of family and friends.

Today, roasts are prepared in the oven – the bird or joint is cooked in a current of air by dry (or radiant) heat. An alternative method is the rôtisserie, which is the modern equivalent of true roasting in medieval Europe. Then, the bird was impaled on a spit and roasted over or in front of an open fire (in fact, true roasting is more like broiling as we know it).

Roasting is only suitable for tender cuts of meat or poultry, as the meat fibers and tissues will shrink and toughen slightly in the initial high temperatures required to seal the outside surfaces. This **sealing** ensures that flavorsome juices will be kept in the bird, providing a moister, full-flavored roast.

Because of its very nature, chicken does not contain a high proportion of fatty tissues and the bird can dry out very quickly during roasting. At one time **larding** the chicken was commonplace. This was done by threading strips of fat (usually bacon) through the flesh. Now, **barding** is recommended – a much simpler method, overlapping strips of fatty bacon along the breast of the chicken. During cooking, the bacon will **baste** the chicken and protect it from drying out. The bacon is removed to one side half an hour before the end of cooking to allow the chicken skin to brown and crispen. (And the bacon is not wasted – it's a delicious accompaniment to the bird.)

Mass-produced chickens will benefit from a forcemeat or stuffing. Tucked inside the body cavity, under the breast skin, or both, a stuffing will add both moisture and flavor to the chicken.

Below is a guide to the oven temperature and cooking times required for the perfect roast chicken.

ROASTING				
Chicken Weight	**Cooking Time**	**Oven Temperature**	**Stuffed Bird**	**Foil Wrapped Bird**
3½ lb. and under	20 mins per lb. + 20 mins extra	375°F	Add 20–25 minutes extra to the overall time	Add 15 minutes extra to the overall time. Pull back the foil for last 20 minutes cooking time to allow chicken to brown.
4–6 lb.	25 mins per lb. + 25 mins extra	325°F		

Foil will help to retain the bird's natural juices, and also cuts down on the need for basting. However, as the chart shows, additional cooking time is required.

Roasting bags help keep the oven clean, and they also self-baste and brown the chicken. They are available in a variety of sizes. It is important to pierce the bag, or cut away a corner, to allow the steam to escape.

Basting as well as barding the chicken breasts with fatty bacon by brushing the chicken with a little oil or melted butter before roasting helps to protect the flesh and crispen the skin. Baste the chicken regularly to keep it moist.

Is the chicken cooked?

Insert a thin skewer into the thickest part of the thigh. If the juices run out clear, then the bird is cooked. Alternatively, tip the chicken up and examine the juices escaping from the body cavity. Again, the juices should be clear.

The leg is also a good indicator: the meat tends to shrink from the end of the drumstick and the leg, when tugged gently away from the body, will "give".

Relaxing

Once any joint or whole bird is cooked, it needs some standing time on a hot dish in a warm place. This allows for all the juices which, during cooking, have drawn up to the surface of the chicken to redistribute back into the flesh. Allow 10 to 15 minutes for this.

POT ROASTING OR BRAISING AND CASSEROLING

Pot roasting is the equivalent of the French method of braising. It is a combination of a type of stew and roast. A pot roast allows you to use older, tougher joints and birds which require longer, slower cooking. A French braising pan or a cast-iron casserole which can be used both over direct heat and in the oven is ideal. These need a tight-fitting lid, otherwise flavoring juices will evaporate and escape.

The principle of pot roasting or braising is to first seal the chicken over a direct heat and then add some herbs, vegetables and just enough stock or wine to cover the vegetables. The liquid will baste and keep the chicken moist, and can then be used in an accompanying sauce. Once the lid is fitted on and the pot roast is transferred to a moderate oven (325°F), the chicken will cook in a moist, steamy atmosphere. The lid may be removed, and the heat increased for a short time towards the end of the cooking period to

brown and roast the surface of the chicken. Cooking time is about 25 per cent longer than roasting.

Casseroling is a long, slow method of cooking chicken and meats in the oven (not to be confused with stewing which takes place on top of the stove). Vegetables, herbs and stock or wine are added to the sealed whole chicken, or portions, and it is then given just enough heat to simmer the liquid gently for as long as is required to tenderize the tougher older bird. A well-fitting lid, again, is important.

SAUTEING, SHALLOW, AND DEEP FAT FRYING

Fried foods have, over the past few years, become taboo. Associations with saturated fats, cholesterol and heart problems have steered the majority of us away to more healthy methods of cooking. However, there are some recipes which cannot, and should not, avoid this method of cooking.

Sautéing is often required to seal chicken portions before transferring them to a casserole dish. This is an excellent method of cooking chicken pieces; it keeps them tender, is easy and quick, and is the healthiest way of savoring "fried" foods.

"Sauté" derives from the French verb *sauter* – to jump. Although the flick of the wrist will not be required to continually toss the chicken (so making it jump), it must be turned frequently to maintain a golden brown color and ensure even cooking. With the range of polyunsaturated fats now available, and good non-stick skillets on the market, sautéed chicken can be included in a healthy eating plan.

Stir-frying has its roots in Oriental cuisine and it is eminently suitable for producing healthy dishes.

Shallow frying requires the chicken portion, coated in seasoned flour or eggs and bread crumbs, to be half submerged in ½ inch hot oil. Use a polyunsaturated oil such as sunflower or corn oil. The result is a crispy outer shell concealing succulent chicken. Turn the chicken half way through cooking. Take care not to over-crowd the pan, as the food will overlap and "steam", and the temperature will lower, causing the food to absorb unnecessary oil.

Deep fat frying. Golden deep fried chicken drumsticks, or the bread crumbed Russian Chicken Kiev concealing mouthwatering buttery, garlicky juices, are enough to cause the most dedicated and calorie-conscious amongst us to waiver.

Deep-fried foods are fattening and often indigestible. The latter is due to the oil being too cool, either from overloading the pan with too much food, or underheating. The protective batter or bread crumb coating on the food will not instantly

seal and, instead, absorbs the oil. The food becomes greasy and soggy, rather than crisp and appetizing. On the other hand, if the oil is too hot, the "shell" will brown too quickly and possibly burn on the outside before cooking the contents. Careful cooking is required at a temperature of between 350 and 375°F, and don't forget the polyunsaturated oil. That will help ease the conscience a little.

BROILING AND BARBECUING

Broiling is a very similar cooking method to roasting, but instead of surrounding the chicken with a dry, intense heat in an oven cavity, broiling radiates heat from one direction – above, or as in the case of a barbecue, below.

Broiling is a delicious method of cooking the most tender, small chickens, game hens and portions. It is a quick method, but requires constant attention, turning the chicken, sealing it on all sides and occasionally basting it. Because the younger chicken may lack maturity, a marinade is an excellent way of adding flavor before cooking. It can also be brushed on the bird as it cooks, to prevent it from drying out.

Barbecuing. When cooking on a barbecue, sprigs of fresh herbs sprinkled on the coals emit appetizing smells.

THE MICROWAVE OVEN

Chickens can be successfully defrosted and cooked in the microwave oven, and once the manufacturer's instructions

MICROWAVE COOKING				
		Cooking Times (minutes)		
Chicken	**Quantity**	**400W**	**500–600W**	**650–700W**
Whole bird. Place breast side down in pierced roasting bag, using rack to keep meat clear of juices. Let sit for 15–20 minutes, wrapped in foil.	1 lb.	12	8	6
	2 lb.	20	14	10
	3½ lb.	28	20	15
	4 lb.	38	26	21
	5 lb.	50	33	26
	6 lb.	62	40	32
Chicken portion with bone*	2 portions	12	8	6
	4 portions	17	13	9
Chicken portion without bone (e.g. breast)**	2 portions	8	5	4
	4 portions	12	8	6

* Arrange in single layer with thinner end towards center.
** Brush with oil or melted butter, turning over once during cooking.

have been carefully read, and the method mastered, the results are moist and tender. However, as with all alternative methods of cooking, a little practice will make perfect. The chart below shows the different cooking times determined by the power of the microwave oven.

THE CHICKEN BRICK

This is a very healthy and under-estimated method of cooking a whole roaster chicken. The chicken is placed in a clay chicken brick (which has previously been soaked in water for 25 minutes), and then simply placed in a preheated oven and cooked for the usual recommended times, but at a high temperature. Because the chicken will cook in its own juices, no added fats or basting is required; the chicken retains its own flavor and nutrients.

PRESSURE COOKING

This is a quick and economical method of cooking chicken, but as with the microwave oven, models vary and instructions must be followed carefully.

STEAMING

Steaming is a quick, natural and healthy way of cooking and an excellent method of retaining nutrients and flavor. This moist method of cooking is ideal for chicken which does have a tendency to dry out easily. An 8 oz. breast will require 20 to 25 minutes, and an 8 oz. leg, 30 to 35 minutes.

ELECTRIC SLOW COOKING

Slow cookers are useful for the person with a hectic lifestyle. It allows long, slow cooking completely unattended. It is the same cooking method, in principle, as braising and casseroling, but sits on the worktop and is plugged in to an electrical power point. The long period of cooking in a moist atmosphere will tenderize the toughest of birds. A 3½ lb. whole chicken will take 4 hours on the high setting to cook, but will sit for another hour without spoiling. Always refer to the manufacturer's instruction book before using.

POACHING

Poaching is carried out in shivering as opposed to simmering water. Because of the low cooking temperature, true poaching is only applicable to fish and eggs.

However, for poultry, the water or stock is kept just under a boil, at a steady simmer. The results, though simple, are delicious. The chicken is moist and tender, any accompanying garden vegetables are full of flavor, and the resulting broth can be made into a wholesome soup or stock.

1

Soups, Appetizers and Starters

Vegetables with Chicken Soup

Serves 6

- 3½ lb. chicken, cut into 8 pieces
- 6¼ pt. chicken stock
- 4 large tomatoes, peeled, seeded and chopped; or 2 x 1 lb. cans chopped tomatoes, drained
- 2 medium-sized corn cobs, cut into 3 inch pieces
- 2 medium yams, peeled and chopped into 1 inch thick slices
- 2 small potatoes, peeled and cut into 1 inch thick slices

- 1 cup peeled and diced pumpkin
- ¾ cup fresh or frozen green peas
- 2 small chiles, seeded and sliced thinly
- 2½ tsp. salt
- freshly ground black pepper
- 1½ tbsp. finely chopped fresh chives

A delicious Caribbean recipe, this soup has its origins in Aruba.

1 Put the chicken pieces and stock into a large saucepan, and bring to a boil over a high heat. Skim off the foam with a large spoon, then reduce the heat, partially cover, and simmer for 45 minutes.

2 Skim the fat from the soup. Add the tomatoes, corn, yams, potatoes, pumpkin, peas, chiles, salt and freshly ground black pepper, and bring to a boil. Reduce the heat, and simmer for about 20 minutes or until the chicken and vegetables are cooked.

3 Taste the soup, adjusting the seasoning if necessary. Stir in the chives, then serve immediately.

'Almost Nothing' Soup

Serves 4-6

- 3½ lb. beef, chicken bones
- 1 onion, unpeeled
- salt and freshly ground black pepper
- 4½ pt. water
- 2 lb. potatoes, scrubbed and dried
- ½ cup bacon fat or melted butter
- 1 large onion, peeled and chopped
- ½ cup light cream (optional)
- **Garnish**
- 2 tbsp. chopped fresh chives

This Russian soup, made from scraps, has a surprising flavor, smoky and nut-like. Add a little cream, to make it more sophisticated.

1 Place the bones, the unpeeled onion, and seasoning to taste in a large pot. Cover with the water, and put over high heat. Bring to a boil, then cover and simmer for 1 hour. Uncover and continue to simmer until the stock has reduced by almost half. Strain the stock and return to the saucepan.

2 Meanwhile peel the potatoes. Reserve the potatoes themselves for another use. Melt the bacon fat or butter in a skillet and sauté the onion until soft, about 6 minutes. Add the potato skins and continue to cook until they too are tender.

3 Transfer the potato skins and onion to the saucepan containing the stock. Bring to a boil, then reduce the heat and simmer for 10 minutes. Purée the soup in batches; return to the saucepan and reheat. Thin, if necessary, with a little water or the cream. Ladle into individual bowls and serve sprinkled with the chopped chives.

Cock-a-Leekie Soup

Serves 4-6

- 1 small chicken, about 2½–3½ lb.
- 1 onion, quartered
- 2 carrots, chopped
- 1 stalk celery, chopped
- 1 bayleaf
- 1 bouquet garni
- 6 peppercorns
- 1 tsp. salt
- 7½ cups water
- 2 tbsp. butter
- 4 leeks, trimmed and thinly sliced
- 2 scallions, trimmed and thinly sliced
- 2 tbsp. long grain rice
- dash allspice
- 1 tbsp. chopped fresh parsley

Scotland is thought to be the home of this substantial soup – although the Welsh may agree to differ! The bird that ended up in the stock pot may originally have been the loser of a cock-fight. Long simmering is required but the result is well worth waiting for.

1 Place the chicken in a large, heavy-based saucepan. Add the onion, carrots, celery, bayleaf, bouquet garni, peppercorns, and salt. Cover with the water.

2 Bring the pan very gently to a boil, skim, and then simmer for about 2 hours or until the chicken is tender. Strain off the stock, discarding the cooked vegetables, and leave to cool, then chill in the refrigerator until the fat hardens and can be easily removed. Alternatively, clean off all the grease from the hot stock with paper towels. Remove the skin from the chicken and cut the flesh into thin strips.

3 Melt the butter in a large pan, add the leeks and scallions and cook over a low heat for 10 minutes. Add the rice and allspice and cook for a further 5 minutes. Pour on the skimmed stock, bring to a boil and simmer for 15 minutes. Add the chicken and simmer for a further 10 minutes, season to taste, mix in the parsley and serve.

Oriental Chicken Noodle Soup

Serves 4-6

- 9 oz. boneless chicken meat (breast or thigh)
- 4 dried Chinese mushrooms
- 5 cups chicken stock
- 2 bundles rice vermicelli noodles, approx. 5 oz.
- 2 tsp. sugar
- 2 tbsp. dark soy sauce
- 3 tbsp. dry sherry or rice wine
- white pepper
- 4 scallions, cut diagonally into 1 inch strips
- 1 tbsp. dried red chili flakes
- 1 tbsp. chopped fresh cilantro
- 2 tsp. sesame oil

Soup is included in almost every meal in Thailand and China and, contrary to Western custom, the soup is eaten together with other dishes, or even at the end of the meal. What is common worldwide, though, is that the basis of a good soup is the stock.

1 Cut the chicken into thin strips. Soak the mushrooms in warm water for 15 minutes. Drain well, squeezing out excess moisture. Cut away and discard the stems, and shred the caps.

2 Bring the chicken stock to a steady simmer. Add the chicken, mushrooms, noodles, sugar, soy sauce, sherry or rice wine, and pepper to taste. Simmer for 15 minutes or until the chicken and noodles are tender.

3 Stir in the scallions, red chili flakes, chopped cilantro, and sesame oil.

4 Pour into individual bowls and serve immediately.

Mulligatawny

Serves 4

- 2 tbsp. vegetable oil
- 1 onion, halved and sliced
- 1 clove garlic, finely chopped
- 1 carrot, peeled and diced
- 1 potato, peeled and diced
- ½ cup trimmed and chopped string or snap beans
- 2 chicken thighs, skinned
- 1 tart eating apple, peeled, cored and diced
- 2 tsp. hot curry paste
- 2 tsp. tomato paste
- ½ tsp. ground ginger
- ½ tsp. grated nutmeg
- 4 cloves
- 3 tbsp. lemon juice
- 1 tbsp. Worcestershire sauce
- 5 cups chicken stock
- salt and freshly ground black pepper

A native of Tamil Nadu, Southern India, the name *milaku* (pepper) and *tanni* (water) is a fitting description of this highly spiced substantial soup. This was one of the many recipes the British Raj brought back to Britain and adapted for "home cooking." Serve accompanied with plain boiled rice.

1 Heat the oil in a large, heavy-based saucepan. Add the onion and garlic and cook for 2–3 minutes, or until the onions start to soften.

2 Add the carrot, potato, beans, and chicken thighs and cook, stirring, for a further 4–5 minutes or until the chicken is lightly colored.

3 Stir in the diced apple, curry paste, tomato paste, ginger, nutmeg, and cloves. Cover and sweat over a moderate heat for 3–4 minutes. Scrape loose any sediment from the base of the pan.

4 Add the lemon juice, Worcestershire sauce and broth. Bring to a boil, then cover and simmer for 20–30 minutes or until the chicken is tender. Season to taste.

5 Lift out the chicken thighs with a slotted spoon. Take the flesh off the bone, break up into small strips and return to the soup.

6 Serve hot. If preferred, the soup can be puréed and served hot or chilled, garnished with a swirl of natural yogurt.

Rice Soup with Chicken

Serves 4

- 6¼ cups chicken stock
- 11 oz. boneless skinned chicken breasts, cut across into thin slices
- 4 cups cooked rice
- ¼ cup chopped pickled cabbage
- 1 tsp. salt
- 1 tsp. ground white pepper
- 1 cup finely sliced celery
- 2 scallions, sliced
- 2 oz. cloves garlic, unpeeled and fried until soft
- 3 oz. sliced red chili with vinegar

The traditional and universal Thai breakfast, tasty and nourishing. It is also made with ground pork, and an optional extra is an egg cracked straight into the dish just before serving; it partly poaches in the hot broth.

1 Boil the chicken stock in a pan. Add the chicken, rice, cabbage, salt and pepper; boil the chicken until cooked, (about 8–10 minutes). Add the celery and scallions, and remove from the heat immediately.

2 Pour into bowls and sprinkle with the fried garlic. Serve with the sliced red chili with vinegar in a separate bowl.

Spicy Chicken Soup

Serves 4

- 1 onion, halved
- 2 stalks celery, including leaves, diced
- 2 carrots, diced
- 1 parsnip, diced
- 5 cloves garlic, peeled
- 3½ lb. chicken
- 6¼ cups water
- ½ tsp. minced fresh basil
- ½ tsp. curry powder
- dash hot pepper sauce
- 1 tsp. minced fresh cilantro
- salt and freshly ground black pepper

This spicy Caribbean-style soup has a well-seasoned, true chicken flavor and the vegetables added toward the end have freshness, color and lots of nutrients. Try adding some of the chicken, shredded or diced, and some noodles for a meal-in-a-dish.

1 Divide the vegetables in half and place in 2 bowls or on sheets of wax paper. Place the garlic, chicken and half the vegetables in a stockpot. Add water to cover the chicken, then the basil, curry powder, hot pepper sauce, cilantro, and salt and pepper to taste. Bring to a boil, then immediately reduce heat and simmer uncovered for about 2 hours.

2 Skim the fat off the top of the stockpot and strain the soup. Refrigerate the cooked chicken for later use.

3 Add the remaining vegetables to the soup. Simmer for another 10 minutes, or until the vegetables are tender, and serve.

Lemon Chicken Soup

Serves 4

- 3–4 lb. free-range chicken, cut into pieces
- 3 cups chicken stock
- 1 medium onion, chopped
- 2 large beef tomatoes, peeled, seeded and chopped
- 1 tbsp. fresh tarragon leaves
- 1 tsp. grated lemon peel
- salt and freshly ground pepper
- 2 potatoes, peeled and chopped
- ½ lb. okra, trimmed
- ½ cup canned chopped jalapeño chiles
- 1 cup frozen corn kernels
- juice of 1 lemon

Garnish

- chopped flat-leaved parsley
- paprika

Chickens in the peasant areas of Lebanon are very much free range and, since they are valued for their eggs, can live to a ripe age (for a chicken!). Older hens find their way into soups like this one.

1 In a large casserole, combine the chicken pieces (except for the breasts), the stock, onion, tomatoes, tarragon, and peel. Pour over 3 cups of water, season to taste, and bring to a boil. Reduce the heat, cover and simmer for 20 minutes. Add the breasts and continue to cook until the breasts are just cooked through. Remove all the chicken pieces from the soup with a slotted spoon and set them aside to cool.

2 Add the potatoes to the soup, cover and continue to simmer until the potatoes are done, about 25 minutes; add the okra after 10 minutes.

3 When the chicken is cool enough to handle, remove the meat from the bones, discarding the skin. Chop the meat into small pieces. Add to the soup, together with the chiles and corn kernels. Bring the soup back to a boil, reduce the heat, and simmer for 5 more minutes. Stir in the lemon juice and serve immediately, garnished with chopped parsley and paprika to taste.

Tlalpeno-style Soup

Serves 4

- 4 oz. chicken (white meat)
- 3¾ cups chicken stock
- 1 or 2 dried red chiles (chili arbole)
- 1–5 cloves garlic
- 3 tbsp. water
- salt to taste (½–1 tsp.)
- 1 avocado

Garnish

- cilantro (about half a handful)

Sometimes the soup is made with a chicken stock; sometimes with vegetable stock. Usually it contains some kind of chili pepper, though which sort of pepper varies widely. Gringo versions usually contain little or no garlic; Mexican versions may contain a whole head. This is a simple, authentic version, for four modest servings.

1 Slice the chicken into julienne strips. If the chicken is not cooked, bring the chicken stock to a boil; simmer the meat until it is cooked (less than 5 minutes). Otherwise, bring the stock and chicken to a simmering boil. Doubling the amount of chicken will not do any harm.

2 De-seed the chiles; tear into pieces; grind in a mortar and pestle with the garlic and 3 tbsp. of water. Strain into the stock. Stir, simmer for a couple of minutes, and add salt to taste.

3 Peel the avocado and slice into strips. Separate the slices carefully before dropping them into the soup, or they will stick together. They will sink for a few moments, then float to the surface. When they do, the soup is ready. Chop some cilantro and float it on the surface for a garnish.

Lime, Tortilla and Salsa Soup

Serves 4

Salsa Cruda (makes 9 oz.)

- 3 large tomatoes, cored and halved
- ¼ cup finely chopped onion
- 2 cloves garlic, minced
- 2 jalapeño chiles, seeded and minced
- 3 tbsp. finely chopped cilantro
- 1 tbsp. olive oil
- 1 tbsp. fresh lime juice
- salt to taste

To make the soup

- 9 oz. Salsa Cruda
- 4¼ cups chicken stock
- 2 tortillas
- 2–3 tbsp. vegetable oil
- 2 half chicken breasts, cooked and shredded
- 2 tbsp. fresh lime juice
- salt to taste

Garnish

- grated Cheddar or dry Mexican cheese

The salsa in this soup is a basic tomato salsa, made with barbecued or broiled tomatoes. It is pleasantly spicy rather than hot, but can be made more piquant if you don't trim away the jalapeño veins and seeds. It can be made several hours in advance.

1 Core the tomatoes, cut them in half and squeeze the seeds out. Place the tomatoes cut side down on a flameproof baking sheet and place them under the broiler. (*Note:* If the baking sheet does not have sides, line it with foil, then crimp the edges to form a shallow bowl to catch the tomato juice.) Broil the tomatoes until the skin is just slightly blackened and loose. Slide off their skins, drain off excess juices, and let them cool.

2 While the tomatoes are cooling, mix together all the remaining ingredients. Then chop the tomatoes and add them to

the salsa. Let sit for 15 minutes or so, then taste and adjust the seasoning.

3 Cut the tortillas into chip-size strips. Heat the oil in a skillet until it is very hot but not smoking. Quickly fry the tortilla strips in batches until they are crisp, 1–2 minutes a side. Drain on paper towels.

4 Put the salsa and chicken stock in a large saucepan. Bring to a boil, reduce the heat and simmer, covered, for 15 minutes. Meanwhile, divide the tortilla chips and shredded chicken between 4 soup bowls.

5 In a blender or food processor, purée the soup in batches. Return the soup to the hob and add the lime and salt to taste. Simmer for about 2 minutes longer for flavors to blend. Pour into the soup bowls, sprinkle cheese on top, and serve immediately.

BELOW: *Homemade Tortilla Chips*

ABOVE: *Salsa Cruda*

Corn, Chicken, and Shrimp Chowder

Serves 4-6

- 2 tbsp. vegetable oil
- 2 medium onions, finely chopped
- 2 medium potatoes, peeled and diced
- 2 dashes grated nutmeg
- 3 cups chicken stock
- salt and freshly ground black pepper
- 2 oz. streaky smoked bacon, rinded and chopped
- 1 half chicken breast, approx. 5 oz., skinned and sliced in strips
- 1 small can, approx. 7 oz., corn kernels, drained
- ⅓ cup shelled shrimp (or 4 scallops, chopped)
- 1¼ cups milk
- 4 tbsp. light cream or fromage frais

Garnish

- freshly chopped chervil

This soup is a meal on its own. The word "chowder" derives from the French Canadian cooking utensil *chaudière*. Originally Newfoundland fishermen made a stew of cod and potatoes, but the recipe developed to include clams, scallops, and salmon. In this version chicken is introduced to the *chaudière*. The combination marries well and makes the shellfish ingredients go further.

1 Heat the oil in a large saucepan and cook the onions for 10 minutes, or until softened, but not browned. Add the diced potato and nutmeg and cook for a further 5 minutes. Stir in the stock, cover and simmer for 15 minutes. Purée in a blender. Season to taste.

2 Fry the bacon in its own fat until well browned. Add the chicken and cook for a further 2 minutes. Stir in the corn kernels, and shrimp or scallops. Add the puréed stock mixture and blend in the milk. Simmer gently for 10 minutes or until the chicken is tender. Season to taste.

3 Serve in deep bowls, garnished with a swirl of cream (or fromage frais) and a dusting of chopped chervil. Accompany with crusty brown bread.

Chicken Livers in Jackets

Makes approx 36

- about ¾ lb. chicken livers
- 16 slices streaky bacon, derinded

To serve
- 1 Chinese gooseberry
- 1 banana
- dried apricot halves (non-soak variety)
- bamboo skewers/toothpicks

Inexpensive to make and quick to produce, these little rolls of crisp bacon encasing chicken livers will soon vanish with the cocktails! The fruits listed here are a suggestion of what to serve with the chicken livers, but almost any fruit works well.

1 Drain the chicken livers, if necessary, and remove any threads. Cut each into pieces the size of a small walnut.

2 Using the back of a heavy knife, stretch the bacon slices lengthwise on a large chopping board. Cut each slice into 2–3 equal lengths, each long enough to wrap around a piece of chicken liver.

3 Roll the bacon lengths around the chicken livers. Push a thin bamboo skewer (pre-soaked for ½ hour to prevent burning) through the center of each roll. Lay on a rack in a broiler pan or small roasting pan.

4 Cook for 10–15 minutes in the oven at 425°F, or under a preheated broiler, until sizzling and crisp. Remove skewers.

5 Meanwhile, prepare the fruit. Cut the banana into thick slices, halve the Chinese gooseberry lengthwise and cut into thick slices.

6 Thread each bacon roll and a piece of fruit onto toothpicks and serve immediately.

Sour Chicken Soup

Serves 8

- 4 lb. chicken
- 1 whole onion, unpeeled
- 1 stalk celery
- 3–4 saffron threads
- 5 black peppercorns, crushed
- dash cayenne pepper
- 3 eggs
- 2 egg yolks
- 2 tbsp. unsalted butter
- 2 onions, finely chopped
- 1 tbsp. flour
- ½ cup fresh lemon juice
- 2 tbsp. finely chopped fresh cilantro
- 2 tbsp. finely chopped fresh parsley
- 1 tbsp. finely chopped fresh mint
- salt and freshly ground black pepper

A traditional Georgian soup, this has echoes of Syria, Israel, and the Indian subcontinent in it. If a thicker, more stew-like result is wanted, the chicken can be shredded into the broth, but this version is more like that commonly encountered in Tbilisi *kafes* and *restorans*.

1 Place the chicken, whole onion, and celery stalk in a heavy saucepan. Add cold water to cover well, and bring to a boil over high heat. Add the saffron, peppercorns, and cayenne pepper to taste, then cover and lower the heat to minimum.

2 Simmer gently for 1½ hours, or until the bird is tender but not falling to pieces. During cooking, skim the scum from the top of the stock occasionally.

3 Transfer the chicken to a dish to drain. Add the juices to the stock. Reserve the bird for another use, serving it with Spiced Walnut Sauce or using it in Russian Chicken and Potato Salad (see page 39).

4 Remove the peppercorns and any bits from the stock with a small sieve, but keep it simmering. In a large bowl, lightly beat together the eggs and egg yolks. Melt the butter in a skillet over medium heat. Sauté the onions until they are softened and just colored, about 6–8 minutes. Add the flour and stir for 3 minutes. Add 1¼ cups stock to the skillet and stir until it begins to thicken. Take off the heat, and allow to rest for 2 minutes, then pour the thickened mixture slowly into the eggs, beating all the time. In turn, pour the egg and stock mixture and the lemon juice into the rest of the stock, beating gently over low heat so that it does not curdle. Stir in the chopped herbs, season the soup to taste, and serve immediately.

Chicken Pho

Serves 4

- 🍲 3 stalks celery, finely chopped
- 🍲 3 scallions, chopped into rings (use green tops as well)
- 🍲 10 oz. cooked chicken, finely shredded
- 🍲 ½ lb. flour sticks or spaghetti noodles
- 🍲 3¾ cups chicken stock or use good-quality bouillon cube
- 🍲 2 pieces light wood ear fungus or 8 white button mushrooms, finely sliced

Traditionally, pho was only made with beef. However, it was recently spotted in Saigon being made with chicken and shrimp. The light wood ear fungi are very nutritious and said to be good for the spirit.

1 Place the celery and scallions in a bowl and put on the table. Place the cooked shredded chicken in a separate bowl and put that on the table also.

2 Follow the instructions on the flour sticks pack, or boil up the spaghetti until just soft. Drain and rinse with some boiling water. Place in 4 bowls.

3 Boil up the chicken stock until simmering, then add the light wood ear fungus or the mushrooms. Place in a bowl and put on the table.

4 The guests should put a mixture of celery, scallion, and shredded chicken onto the noodles then ladle the hot chicken broth into the bowls.

Sicilian Tomatoes

Serves 4-8

- 8 beef tomatoes
- 2 tbsp. olive oil
- 1 medium onion, finely chopped
- 1 clove garlic, minced
- ½ oz. pinenuts
- 1 cup fresh white bread crumbs
- 1 cup finely chopped or minced cooked chicken
- 2 tbsp. fresh marjoram
- 2 tsp. capers, chopped
- 4 black olives, chopped
- salt and freshly ground pepper
- dash hot pepper sauce
- ¼ cup freshly grated Parmesan cheese

Firm, round beef tomatoes are perfect for stuffing with the flavors of the Mediterranean, either as a starter or a supper dish. Try tuna fish as an alternative to chicken.

1 Slice the top off each tomato and scoop out the pulp and seeds; chop and reserve these for later use.

2 Heat the oil in a pan and gently cook the onion and garlic and pinenuts, until the onion is softened and the nuts golden brown.

3 Stir in the bread crumbs and chicken. Cook for a further minute. Remove from the heat and stir in the marjoram, capers, olives and salt and pepper to taste. Stir in the tomato pulp and add a dash of hot pepper sauce.

4 Spoon the stuffing mixture back into the tomato shells. Sprinkle with the Parmesan cheese.

5 Place the tomatoes on a greased baking sheet and cook for 20–30 minutes at 350°F or until tender and the Parmesan is golden. Serve warm.

Chicken and Scallion Canâpés

Makes 35–40

- 2 boneless half chicken breasts, skinned, approx. 6 oz. each
- 1 bunch scallions, trimmed

Marinade
- 4 tbsp. light soy sauce
- 2 tbsp. sherry vinegar

Garnish
- chili flowers (optional)
- fresh cilantro or dill

These canâpés are straightforward, disappear as quickly as they are made, and are low in calories too!

1 Halve the chicken breasts, put each between 2 sheets of dampened wax paper and flatten to a thickness of ½ inch. Halve each piece lengthwise, to give a total of 8 pieces.

2 Place a scallion lengthwise on each chicken piece, and roll up tightly. Secure with cotton or string.

3 Mix together the marinade ingredients in a shallow dish and add the chicken rolls. Cover and chill for 2–3 hours, turning the rolls occasionally.

4 Steam the chicken rolls for 5 minutes, or cook in a 650W microwave oven for 4–5 minutes on HIGH. (Position the rolls around the outer edge of a large plate.)

5 Return the cooked chicken to the marinade to cool for 1 hour, turning frequently to coat them.

6 Remove the string and cut the rolls at a diagonal into ½ inch slices. Dust with paprika and arrange on a serving platter. Garnish with some chili flowers if you like and sprigs of fresh cilantro or dill.

Filo Chicken Rolls

Serves 8-10

- 🪶 1 lb. chicken breast, skinned
- 🪶 1 large onion, quartered
- 🪶 2 stalks celery, roughly chopped
- 🪶 3 peppercorns
- 🪶 dash salt
- 🪶 sprig of fresh parsley
- 🪶 ¼ cup butter
- 🪶 2 tbsp. chopped fresh dill
- 🪶 ½ cup grated feta cheese
- 🪶 1 egg, beaten
- 🪶 ½ lb. filo pastry, thawed if frozen
- 🪶 1 cup melted butter

Filo pastry is widely used in Greek cookery and so long as a few simple rules are followed, it is easy to work with and the results are always impressive.

1 Place the chicken in a deep skillet with the onion, celery, peppercorns, salt, and parsley sprigs. Add enough water to cover the chicken and simmer for 20–25 minutes, or until the chicken is cooked through.

2 Remove the chicken from the pan using a slotted spoon and transfer to a food processor or blender with the onion and celery. Discard the cooking liquid and clean the pan ready to use again.

3 Process the chicken and vegetables until the texture is fine. Melt ¼ cup butter in the cleaned skillet and sauté the chicken and vegetable mixture for 5–10 minutes, or until lightly browned. Stir in the chopped dill and the grated cheese. Set aside to cool completely, then beat in the egg. Preheat the oven to 375°F.

4 To make the filo rolls lay the filo pastry out on the work surface and cover with a slightly damp cloth. Separate the first sheet of pastry and lay it on the work surface, keeping the remaining sheets covered to prevent them from drying out. Divide into three equal strips and brush each strip lightly with the melted butter.

5 Place 2 heaped teaspoons of the chicken mixture at one end of the strip of pastry and fold in the long sides of the strip by about ¼ inch. Roll up the pastry strip, starting at the filling end, keeping the roll firm and neat. Place the roll on a buttered baking sheet and brush with a little extra melted butter.

6 Repeat the process with the other strips and then continue with another sheet of pastry in the same way. You may need more than one buttered baking sheet.

7 Bake the filo rolls in the oven for about 20 minutes, or until lightly golden and crisp.

Rice and Chicken Croquettes

Makes 24

- 1 lb. cooked, diced chicken
- 1 lb. cooked rice
- ½ onion, chopped
- 2 tsp. tomato catsup
- salt and freshly ground black pepper
- ½ tsp. paprika
- 3 eggs, beaten
- ½ cup dried bread crumbs
- vegetable oil for frying

These easily-made croquettes make a delicious starter or light snack.

1 Mix all the ingredients together, except the eggs, bread crumbs, and oil. Roll the mixture into small balls, then dip each one in the beaten egg and roll in the bread crumbs to coat them.

2 Heat some oil in a saucepan and deep-fry the croquettes until they are golden brown. Serve at once with hot pepper sauce on the side.

Country Mushrooms

Serves 4 or 8

- 8 large flat mushrooms
- 1 tbsp. sunflower oil plus a little extra
- 1 small onion, finely chopped
- 1 clove garlic, finely chopped
- 4 oz. boneless chicken (thigh or breast)
- 2 slices lean smoked bacon, derinded
- 2 cups fresh white bread crumbs
- 1 tbsp. Worcestershire sauce
- good dash mustard powder
- salt and freshly ground black pepper
- 1 egg, beaten
- scant ½ cup freshly grated Parmesan cheese
- 2 tbsp. milk

Garnish

- chopped fresh parsley

Large open field mushrooms are full of flavor on their own, but are also good topped with this savory stuffing for a starter or light meal. Chicken livers could be used instead of chicken.

1 Remove the stems from the mushrooms and chop finely.

2 Heat the oil in a pan, and sauté the onions and garlic until softened. Add the chopped mushroom stems and cook for a further minute.

3 Finely dice the chicken and bacon and add to the pan. Stir-fry for a further 2 minutes. Remove from the heat and mix in the bread crumbs, Worcestershire sauce, mustard and seasonings. Stir in the beaten egg.

4 Spoon the mixture into the mushroom caps to form neat heaps.

5 Drizzle a small amount of oil over the top of each filled mushroom and then sprinkle with a little Parmesan cheese.

6 Place the mushrooms on a large, lightly oiled baking sheet. Add the milk to prevent the mushrooms from drying out.

7 Bake for 20 minutes at 400°F. Serve hot, sprinkled liberally with chopped parsley.

Carrot and Chicken Timbales with Sweet Pepper Sauce

Serves 6

- 6 oz. cooked chicken breast
- 1½ cups low fat cream cheese or fromage frais
- 2 large eggs plus 1 egg yolk
- salt and white pepper
- 1½ cups cooked and chopped carrots
- ½ tsp. ground coriander

Sauce

- 2 large sweet red or yellow bell peppers
- 1 small shallot or ½ a small sweet onion, finely chopped
- 1 clove garlic, finely chopped
- 2 cups vegetable or chicken stock
- dash sugar
- salt and pepper, to taste

Garnish

- fresh chervil
- baby carrots with leaves, when available

A bright and colorful start to a meal, best served just warm. The sauce can be made well in advance and chilled until required, but the delicate creamy timbales are ideally eaten freshly made.

If you have the time, divide the sauce ingredients and make one half with red and the other half with yellow peppers.

1 Put the chicken, half the cheese and one egg in a good processor or blender and process until smooth. Season to taste. Transfer to a small bowl.

2 Repeat the process with the carrots, the remaining cheese and egg and the egg yolk. Season to taste and stir in the ground coriander.

3 Lightly grease 6 small timbale (thimble-shaped) molds and divide half the chicken mixture between the bases of each mold. Then spoon on the carrot purée and finally the remaining chicken mixture. Tap the side of each mold gently to level out the surface.

4 Place the molds in a roasting tin half filled with water, cover with foil and cook for 40 minutes or until lightly set. (A wooden toothpick will come out of the mousse clean when it is cooked.) Leave to stand for 5 minutes before unmolding.

5 Meanwhile, make the sauce. Cut the peppers into pieces. Sweat the onions and garlic in a covered pan with a couple of tablespoons of stock. (Do not brown the onions.)

6 Add the peppers and stock and simmer, uncovered, for 15–20 minutes or until the peppers are tender. Blend to a smooth purée and season to taste with salt, pepper and sugar. Leave to cool slightly.

7 Spoon the warm sauce over a plate. (If you are using two colors, spoon one sauce on one side of the plate and the second color on the other side. Gently tip the plate just enough to run the sauces into one another.)

8 Carefully unmold the timbales and place in the center of each plate. Garnish with sprigs of fresh chervil and a small baby carrot, and serve immediately.

Quenelles of Chicken with Sorrel Sauce

Serves 4

- 13 oz. chicken breast, skinned
- 1 egg plus 1 egg white
- ½ cup fromage frais or heavy cream
- salt and freshly ground pepper
- 1 tbsp. chopped fresh chives
- 5 cups chicken stock

Sauce

- ½ lb. sorrel leaves
- 1½ cups chicken stock
- 4 tbsp. fromage frais
- salt and freshly ground black pepper

Garnish

- fresh chives

Quenelles are small, egg-shapes of a mousse-like, finely ground meat mixture, poached in a simmering liquid. The quenelle mixture can be prepared in advance, but must be cooked at the very last moment. Vary the sauce according to the availability of fresh herbs. Tarragon, mixed herbs, even watercress, are equally good.

1 Cut up the chicken and put it into a food processor and work until finely chopped.

2 Season, add the egg and egg white and process again until smooth. Fold in the fromage frais and chives. Adjust the seasoning, turn onto a wetted plate and chill for 3–4 hours.

3 Meanwhile, make the sauce. Remove the larger stems from the sorrel and blanch the leaves in ½ cup boiling stock. Allow to cool, then purée in a blender together with the fromage frais. Season to taste.

4 Boil the remaining stock until reduced by half. Stir into the sorrel sauce, and keep warm.

5 To make the quenelles, mold the chilled chicken into oval shapes by using 2 wet dessertspoons. Bring the 5 cups stock to a simmer in a large skillet. Gently slide each quenelle into the simmering stock and poach for about 2 minutes on each side. Drain on paper towels.

6 Spoon the warmed sauce onto 4 individual plates, top with the quenelles and garnish with fresh chives. Serve immediately.

Chicken Nuggets

Makes approx. 18

- 1 lb. boneless chicken, minced
- 1 cup fresh white bread crumbs
- 4 tbsp. mango chutney
- 1 small onion, finely chopped
- 1 tsp. ground coriander
- salt and freshly ground black pepper
- 1 egg, lightly beaten
- 2 tbsp. wholewheat flour
- 2 tbsp. vegetable oil

Good enough on their own as a cocktail snack, or served with a relish and salad. For a more substantial nugget, replace bread crumbs with cooked rice.

1 In a large bowl, combine the chicken, bread crumbs, chutney, onion, coriander, and seasonings. Add enough beaten egg to bind the ingredients together.

2 Shape the mixture into small nuggets the size of a cork. Dust lightly with the wholewheat flour.

3 Heat the oil in a large skillet and cook the nuggets for 10–15 minutes, turning frequently, until golden brown. Serve hot or cold.

Crunchy Nut Drumsticks

Makes 12

- 2 cups fresh white bread crumbs
- 4 tbsp. salted peanuts, finely chopped
- 2 tbsp. chopped fresh parsley
- 1 tsp. dried garlic granules
- ½ tsp. curry powder
- ½ tsp. paprika
- 12 chicken drumsticks
- 2 eggs, beaten
- 3 tbsp. peanut oil

Mexican Dip
- 3 tbsp. grated onion
- 3 tbsp. white wine vinegar
- ⅔ cup tomato catsup
- 1 tsp. Worcestershire sauce
- juice of ½ lemon
- ½ tsp. paprika
- salt

Garnish
- 1 scallion, trimmed and finely sliced

Avocado Dip
- 1 ripe avocado, peeled and pitted
- 1 tbsp. lemon juice
- ⅔ cup low calorie mayonnaise
- dash hot pepper sauce
- salt
- paprika

Children and adults alike will enjoy these crunchy drumsticks, especially when partnered with contrasting dips.

1 Mix together the bread crumbs, peanuts, parsley, garlic granules, curry powder, and paprika.

2 Dip the drumsticks into the beaten egg, drain well, then coat with the bread crumb mixture.

3 Place the drumsticks in a large shallow roasting pan. Drizzle over the peanut oil, and then cook for 40 minutes at 350°F until golden brown and crisp.

4 Meanwhile make the dips. For the Mexican Dip, simmer the onion and vinegar in a small pan for 5 minutes. Stir in the remaining ingredients. Simmer for a couple of minutes more. Season to taste. Serve garnished with finely sliced scallion.

5 For the Avocado Dip, put all the ingredients, except the paprika, in a food processor or blender and blend until smooth. Season to taste. Serve sprinkled with paprika.

Chicken Liver Pâté

Serves 4

- 1 lb. chicken livers
- 6 tbsp. ruby port
- 2 cloves garlic, minced
- 2 tsp. chopped fresh thyme
- ½ tsp. grated nutmeg
- 2 tbsp. butter
- 4 tbsp. fromage frais or heavy cream
- salt and freshly ground black pepper
- 1 tsp. gelatin powder
- ⅔ cup chicken stock

Garnish

- bayleaves
- peppercorns
- stuffed olives

A very good pâté – quick to make and best served with melba toast or french bread. Try it too, as a canapé, spooned into small mushroom caps or hollowed out cherry tomatoes.

1 Trim and wash the livers, and cut in half. Put them in a bowl with the port, garlic, thyme, and nutmeg. Mix the ingredients well, cover and marinate for 2 hours. Drain the livers, reserving the juices.

2 Melt the butter in a skillet, add the drained livers, and sauté for a few minutes or until the livers change color.

3 Add the reserved juices and simmer, uncovered, for a further minute. Cool slightly. Season to taste.

4 Blend or process the liver mixture together with the fromage frais or cream until smooth. Pour into a small serving dish (or 4 individual ramekin dishes). Cover and place in a roasting pan half filled with water. Cook for 40 minutes at 350°F.

5 Sprinkle the gelatin into the hot chicken stock. Dissolve over a pan of hot water (or microwave on HIGH at 600W for 30 seconds). Cool to room temperature, or until just syrupy.

6 Arrange the bayleaves, peppercorns, and stuffed olive slices on top of the pâté. Carefully spoon a thin layer of the gelatin mixture over. Chill until set.
Note: the made up pâté will freeze for up to 2 months, after cooking, but before the gelatin is applied.

Curried Chicken Salad in Puffs

Makes 24-30 small puffs

- 1 cup milk
- 5 tbsp. butter
- dash salt
- 1 cup all-purpose flour
- 4 eggs at room temperature

Curried Chicken Salad

- ¾ lb. cooked chicken, cut into strips
- 1 large or 2 small peaches, peeled and cubed
- ½ cup small seedless grapes
- ¼ cup slivered almonds
- 2 tbsp. chopped scallions
- ¼ cup chopped celery
- ⅓ cup mayonnaise
- ⅓ cup sour cream
- 2 tsp. curry powder
- ¼ tsp. salt

Here, cream puff shells are filled with chicken salad for delicious hors d'oeuvres or picnic finger food. Try other savory fillings, such as crab or ham salad. The puffs and salad can be made early in the day, then assembled about an hour before serving.

1 Preheat the oven to 400°F. Cover two baking sheets with foil or wax paper, then grease the paper.

2 Bring the milk, butter, and salt to a boil in a medium saucepan. Add all the flour at once. Stir constantly until the mixture turns into a thick dough that pulls away from the sides of the pan. Remove from heat. Add one egg at a time, beating the dough with a wooden spoon until each egg is fully incorporated before adding the next.

3 Using a spoon or a pastry bag, form the dough into walnut-sized balls. Place the balls on the baking sheets. Bake for 10 minutes at 400°F, then reduce the heat to 350°F and bake until the puffs are golden brown, about 25 minutes. Cool away from any drafts. When the puffs are cool, slice off the tops with a sharp knife. Remove any soft center from inside. Fill with chicken salad and replace the tops. Keep refrigerated until serving time.

4 Now to the salad. If the peaches are very juicy, set them in a colander to drain while you mix the other ingredients. Or go ahead and put them in the salad; you'll just have a juicier salad.

5 Combine the chicken, peaches, grapes, almonds, onions, and celery in a medium bowl. In a separate bowl, mix the mayonnaise, sour cream, curry powder, and salt. Add the dressing to the salad and mix thoroughly. If the salad seems dry, add a little mayonnaise.

6 To avoid soggy puffs, fill the puffs with the salad no more than 1 hour before serving time.

Chicken Tostada

Serves 6

- 6 regular-size tostada shells
- oil or shortening for frying
- 1 small skinned, boneless half chicken breast
- ½ lettuce
- 3 tomatoes
- ½ cup sour cream

Beans

- 1 lb. canned kidney beans
- 1 onion, chopped
- 2 servano chiles
- 2 cloves garlic
- 1 tomato, peeled, seeded and chopped
- salt and pepper to taste

This dish looks pretty garnished with sliced red or green scallions; slices of avocado; olives; and, for color, a dash of paprika.

1 Boil the chicken breast until it is soft enough to be shredded with two forks – anything up to an hour. Shred.

2 Fry the tostada shells in the oil or shortening until crisp – or use ready-made tostada shells.

3 Fry beans ingredients until soft and mash.

4 Top the tostada shells with a generous layer of beans mixture, about 2–3 tablespoons per tortilla. On top of this, place one-sixth of the shredded chicken. Next, add the shredded lettuce; sliced tomato; and sour cream.

Lentil and Chicken Loaf

Serves 6

- generous 1 cup lentils
- 1 sprig fresh sage
- 1 small onion, studded with 4 cloves
- 1 clove garlic, minced
- 1 medium onion, finely chopped
- ¼ cup Cheddar cheese, grated
- ⅔ cup low fat yogurt
- 2 eggs, beaten
- 1 tbsp. chopped fresh sage
- 1 cup finely chopped cooked chicken
- salt and freshly ground black pepper

Serve this loaf hot or cold, accompanied with your favorite fresh tomato sauce.

1 Soak the lentils in cold water overnight. Drain, and put in a pan with sufficient cold water to cover. Add the sprig of sage, the small onion with cloves, and the garlic. Bring to a boil, then cover and cook for 25–30 minutes or until the lentils are tender. Drain, discarding the sage and the onion.

2 Mix the cooked lentils with the chopped onion, cheese, yogurt, eggs, chopped sage, chicken, and season to taste.

3 Pour into a greased and base-lined 2 lb. loaf pan, and smooth the surface level. Cook for 1 hour at 350°F. Allow to cool in the pan for 10 minutes before turning out. Cut into slices to serve.

Spinach, Chicken and Smoked Salmon Roulade

Serves 4

- 4 oz. fresh spinach
- 4 boneless half chicken breasts, skinned, approx. 6 oz. each
- 2 oz. smoked salmon slivers (or trimmings)
- ½ lemon, finely grated rind
- salt and freshly ground black pepper
- 3 tbsp. sunflower oil
- 6 tbsp. low calorie mayonnaise
- 1 tbsp. chopped fresh dill

Garnish

- sprigs of dill

These attractive "pinwheels," accompanied by a dill mayonnaise and a crisp salad, are ideal for a summer lunch or picnic.

1 Remove the thick stem part from each spinach leaf. Blanch spinach in boiling water for 1 minute, refresh in cold water and drain on paper towels.

2 Place each chicken breast between 2 sheets dampened wax paper and flatten to approximately ½ inch thick, with a rolling pin. (Try to keep as neat a shape as possible.)

3 Lay the drained spinach leaves over each chicken breast, smooth side down, then lay the smoked salmon on top and sprinkle over the grated lemon rind. Season to taste.

4 Roll up, jelly roll fashion, and secure with wooden toothpicks.

5 Heat the oil in a shallow pan; add the chicken roulades and cook gently for 20 minutes, turning them occasionally until the chicken is tender.

6 Allow to cool, then remove the toothpicks and wrap the cooked roulades in plastic wrap. Chill until required.

7 To serve, slice the roulades and accompany with the mayonnaise, to which has been added the chopped dill, seasoned to taste. Garnish with dill sprigs.

Pork, Chicken, and Walnut Terrine

Serves 6-8

- *9 oz. chicken livers*
- *1 tbsp. vegetable oil*
- *¼ lb. chicken breast, skinned*
- *2 tbsp. medium sherry*
- *1 tbsp. brandy*
- *a few black peppercorns, roughly crushed*
- *1 lb. ground pork*
- *1 egg*
- *1 clove garlic, minced*
- *1 tsp. salt*
- *4 tbsp. coarsely chopped walnuts*

Garnish

- *assorted salad leaves*
- *scallion flowers (optional)*

The French word "terrine" originally meant an earthenware dish, but nowadays refers to its contents. This needs to be made a day or two in advance to develop the flavors, and should be served cold, sliced, with a salad garnish and wholewheat bread.

1 Sauté half the chicken liver in the oil until just browned. Remove and cut into thin strips. Cut the chicken breast into thin strips and put in a bowl with the cooked livers, the sherry, brandy, and peppercorns. Cover and leave to marinate for 2 hours.

2 Put the remaining chicken livers and the pork in a food processor and blend together with the egg, garlic, and salt, until the mixture is smooth.

3 Place one third of this mixture in a lightly greased 2 pt. terrine or loaf pan, and cover with half the chicken strips and half the walnuts.

4 Cover with another third of the pork mixture, and then the rest of the chicken strips and walnuts. Spread the remaining pork mixture over the top. Cover with foil.

5 Place on a baking sheet, and bake for 1 hour at 375°F. Cool, top off any liquid and then chill, preferably overnight.

6 Serve in slices, garnished with an assortment of salad leaves and, if you like, scallion flowers.

Avocado and Chicken Quiche

Serves 6

- *9 oz. basic pie dough*
- *1 small onion, finely chopped*
- *1 tbsp. sunflower oil*
- *9 oz. cooked chicken, finely chopped*
- *1 firm avocado pear, peeled, pitted and cubed*
- *6 tbsp. low fat cream cheese, cut into small knobs*
- *1 tbsp. each freshly chopped tarragon, parsley, and chives*
- *3 eggs*
- *⅞ cup milk*
- *salt and freshly ground black pepper*

Garnish

- *thin slivers of peeled avocado dipped in lemon juice*
- *chopped fresh parsley or chives*

Try the subtle combination of chicken, avocado and cream cheese. Zucchini sliced and blanched make a good alternative to avocado if you prefer.

1 Roll out the pastry fairly thinly and use to line a 9 inch diameter loose-bottomed fluted flan ring. Place on a baking sheet. Fill with a circle of wax paper and baking beans. Bake "blind" for 10–15 minutes at 375°F.

2 Cook the onion gently in the oil for 3–4 minutes. Scatter over the base of the pastry shell. Add the chicken, avocado, cream cheese, and herbs.

3 Beat together the eggs, milk, and seasoning, to taste. Pour into the pastry shell. Cook for 35 minutes or until the filling is set.

4 Serve either warm or cold, garnished with slices of avocado and freshly chopped herbs.

Spinach and Chicken Terrine

Serves 8-10

Spinach Mixture

- *1 lb. cooked spinach, well drained and chopped*
- *freshly grated nutmeg*
- *salt and freshly ground black pepper*
- *⅔ cup fromage frais (low fat)*
- *2 egg yolks*
- *2 tsp. gelatin powder*

Chicken Mixture

- *1 tbsp. vegetable oil*
- *1½ lb. boneless chicken, ground*
- *1 clove garlic, minced*
- *1 tsp. green peppercorns*
- *salt and freshly ground black pepper*
- *4 tbsp. dry Vermouth*
- *¼ cup pistachio nuts*
- *¾ cup fromage frais (low fat)*
- *3 tsp. gelatin powder*

Sauce

- *⅞ cup thick natural yogurt (preferably low fat)*
- *1 bunch watercress, washed and trimmed*
- *1 whole clove garlic, peeled*
- *4 tbsp. dry white wine*
- *salt and freshly ground black pepper*

Garnish

- *a few green peppercorns or a sprig of dill*

A perfect start to a dinner party, or as a main course for a summer lunch. Serve on its own, or with new potatoes and a fresh crisp green salad.

1 For the spinach mixture, mix the spinach with nutmeg, salt and pepper to taste. Blend in the fromage frais and egg yolks.

2 Dissolve the gelatin in 2 tbsp. water (place in a bowl over a pan of simmering water). Allow to cool slightly before stirring into the spinach mixture.

3 For the chicken mixture, heat the oil and stir-fry the ground chicken for 4–5 minutes. Do not allow it to brown.

4 Add the garlic, green peppercorns, salt and pepper to taste, and the Vermouth. Bubble briskly for 1 minute.

5 Blend the chicken in a blender or food processor until smooth. Stir the pistachio nuts and fromage frais into the chicken mixture.

6 Dissolve the gelatin in 3 tbsp. water (as above) and add to the chicken mixture; blend well.

7 Put half the chicken mixture into a lightly oiled and lined 2 lb. loaf pan, cover carefully with the spinach mixture, and spread the remaining chicken mixture over the top. Chill until the terrine is firm enough to slice.

8 Meanwhile, make the sauce. Put the yogurt, watercress and garlic into a blender or food processor and blend until smooth. Stir in the white wine and season to taste.

9 Carefully unmold the set terrine and cut into slices. Place a slice on each serving plate, and spoon a pool of sauce around the terrine. Garnish with a few extra green peppercorns or a sprig of fresh dill.

Raised Chicken and Ham Pie

Serves 8

- ❧ hot water crust dough made with 1 lb. all-purpose flour
- ❧ 750 g (1½ lb) chicken breast, skinned and diced
- ❧ 1 lb. gammon (raw smoked ham), diced
- ❧ ¼ lb. streaky bacon, rinded and diced
- ❧ 4 tbsp. chopped parsley
- ❧ 1 tsp. chopped fresh thyme
- ❧ 1 tsp. green peppercorns, coarsely chopped
- ❧ dash grated nutmeg
- ❧ 4 tbsp. dry white wine
- ❧ 2 tbsp. butter
- ❧ 1 egg, beaten, to glaze
- ❧ 1¼ cups chicken stock
- ❧ 1 tbsp. gelatin powder

A raised pie is a must for outdoor eating. It is easy to pack and carry and excellent accompanied with some cranberry or red currant jelly. Although special raised pie pans are available, in this case a deep loose-bottomed cake pan can be used.

1 Lightly grease a deep 7 inch cake pan with removable base. Roll out two thirds of the pastry to ¼ inch thick. Line the cake pan.

2 In a bowl, mix together the chicken, ham, bacon, parsley, thyme, peppercorns, and nutmeg. Spoon into the pie shell. Pour over the wine and dot with butter.

3 Roll the remaining pastry into an 7 inch round. Brush the edges of the pie with some of the beaten egg. Cover with the circle of pastry and crimp the edges to seal.

4 Glaze the top of the pie with more beaten egg. Cut a cross in the center and lift up the pastry to form a small vent. Insert a small aluminum foil funnel into the hole.

Oriental Chicken Salad

Serves 4

- ❧ 4 half chicken breasts, approx. 5 oz. each, skinned and boned
- ❧ 1¼ cups chicken stock or dry white wine

Marinade
- ❧ 2 tbsp. teriyaki marinade (or soy sauce)
- ❧ 1 tbsp. dry sherry
- ❧ 1 tbsp. clear honey
- ❧ 1 tsp. grated fresh ginger
- ❧ 1 clove garlic, minced
- ❧ ½ sweet red bell pepper, seeded and cut into strips
- ❧ 1 small carrot, cut into thin strips
- ❧ 4 scallions, trimmed and halved lengthwise
- ❧ 1 stalk celery, chopped
- ❧ 4 water chestnuts (canned), sliced
- ❧ 4 baby corn, blanched and halved lengthwise

- ❧ 1 tbsp. sesame seeds, toasted

Dressing
- ❧ 2 tbsp. sherry vinegar
- ❧ 2 tbsp. vegetable oil
- ❧ 1 tbsp. teriyaki marinade (or soy sauce)
- ❧ 1 tbsp. dry sherry
- ❧ 1 tbsp. stem ginger syrup
- ❧ ½ tsp. sesame oil

This salad can be prepared up to 12 hours in advance and is an ideal lunch dish or one to include in a buffet table – in which case this quantity would serve 8 to 10.

5 Re-roll the pastry trimmings. Cut into leaves or tassles. Arrange on top of the pie. Glaze with the remaining beaten egg.

6 Bake at 450°F oven setting for 20 minutes, then reduce to 325°F and cook for 2 hours. Cover with aluminum foil to prevent the pastry from becoming too brown. Remove the foil 20 minutes before the end to crispen the pastry.

7 Heat the stock in a saucepan. Sprinkle over the gelatin and stir over a gentle heat, until the gelatin has completely dissolved. Pour a little at a time through the funnel into the cooked pie.

8 Cool the pie in the pan, then chill thoroughly. Turn out of the pan and serve.

1 Place the chicken in a shallow dish. Put the marinade ingredients in a screw top jar. Shake vigorously, then pour onto the chicken. Cover and chill for several hours.

2 Remove the chicken with a slotted spoon; discard the marinade. Put the stock in a small pan, add the chicken, cover and simmer for 10 minutes or until tender. Drain and cool the chicken, then cut into thin strips.

3 Combine the chicken with the vegetable and salad ingredients. Sprinkle over the sesame seeds.

4 Shake the dressing ingredients together in a screw top jar and pour over the chicken salad. Serve.

Chicken Rice Salad with Chili Salsa

Serves 4-6

- 1¼ lb. cooked white rice
- 2 half chicken breasts, cooked and cubed
- 9 oz. Hot Salsa (see below)
- ¼ cup chopped scallions
- 1½ oz. toasted slivered almonds
- 1 avocado, peeled, pitted and diced
- 1 tbsp. red wine vinegar
- salt to taste

Chilli Salsa (makes about 1¼ lb.)

- 4 large tomatoes, seeded and chopped
- ¾ cup chopped sweet bell pepper
- ½ cup chopped red onion
- ⅓ cup chopped scallions
- 3 jalapeño chiles, seeded and chopped
- 3 tbsp. chopped fresh cilantro
- 2 cloves garlic, minced
- 1 tbsp. fresh lime juice
- salt and pepper to taste

Serve this chunky hot salsa salad on a bed of lettuce for a delicious luncheon dish. It is best when the chicken is marinated and broiled, but any cooked chicken will do. The salsa is good with corn chips, or as a topping for eggs and soups, or mixed into vegetables.

1 Combine all the Chilli Salsa ingredients. Let sit for about 15 minutes, then taste and adjust the salt and pepper.

2 Combine all the salad ingredients. Taste and adjust the seasonings.

3 To toast almonds: spread them in a single layer on a small baking sheet. Bake at 350°F until golden brown, 7–10 minutes.

Orange, Endive and Chicken Salad

Serves 4

- 9 oz. brown rice
- 1 tbsp. olive oil
- 1 tbsp. chopped fresh tarragon (or parsley)
- grated rind and juice of 1 large orange
- ⅔ cup low fat yogurt
- ¼ cup low fat cream cheese
- 1 lb. cooked chicken, cubed
- ¼ cup slivered almonds, toasted
- 1 tbsp. snipped fresh chives
- 2 tsp. coriander seeds, crushed
- salt and freshly ground black pepper
- 2–3 heads Belgian endive

Garnish

- julienne of orange rind
- fresh tarragon or parsley

Buy either red or green Belgian endive for this recipe – the leaves can be used as scoops to eat the salad. Serve on its own or with a simple tomato salad.

1 Cook the rice according to instructions. Drain thoroughly and fork in the olive oil, fresh tarragon, orange juice, and ½ tsp. of the orange rind. Let cool. Cover and chill.

2 Beat the yogurt and cream cheese together with ½ tsp. orange rind. Fold in the chicken, toasted almonds, chives, coriander seeds, and season with salt and pepper to taste. Cover and chill.

3 Arrange the Belgian endive leaves around the outer edge of a shallow round serving dish. Spoon a circle of rice around the base of the endive and pile the chicken mixture in the center.

4 Garnish with julienne strips of orange rind and sprigs of fresh tarragon.

Negombo Pineapple and Chicken Salad

Serves 2-4

- 1 medium pineapple
- 3 tbsp. low calorie mayonnaise
- 1 tbsp. mild curry powder
- ½ tsp. ground cumin
- ½ lb. cooked chicken, cubed
- 2 stalks celery, diced
- 2 scallions, trimmed and chopped
- 1 medium potato, boiled and cubed
- 1 tart eating apple, peeled, cored, and diced
- 1 tbsp. coconut flakes, toasted
- 6 cardamon pods, seeds only, lightly crushed
- 1 tbsp. chopped fresh cilantro
- ⅔ cup low fat natural yogurt
- salt and freshly ground black pepper

Garnish

- 1 tomato, skinned, seeded and cut into strips
- fresh cilantro sprigs

Named after a village in "Paradise" – Sri Lanka – abundant with fresh sweet pineapples, coconuts, and spice plantations. Serve as a light lunch, or part of a buffet, accompanied with poppadums.

1 Halve the pineapple (and leafy top) lengthwise. Carefully scoop out the flesh, cut into neat cubes and place in a large bowl. Reserve the shells.

2 Blend the mayonnaise, curry powder, and cumin together and gently fold into the pineapple with the remaining ingredients. Season to taste. Cover and chill for 2 hours, to allow the flavors to develop.

3 Divide the mixture between the two pineapple shells, and serve garnished with the strips of tomato and fresh cilantro sprigs.

Fried Chicken Salad

Serves 4

- 4 half chicken breasts, boneless
- 1 cup flour
- ½ tsp. salt
- 1 tsp. paprika
- ½ tsp. black pepper
- ½ tsp. dried thyme
- ¼ tsp. celery salt
- oil for frying

Salad

- 5–6 oz. lettuce leaves, any type, torn
- 1 cup sliced mushrooms
- 2 stalks celery, diced
- 2 scallions, chopped
- pitted black olives

Make salad into a main dish with the addition of warm strips of fried chicken. For ease of cooking and slicing, use boneless chicken breasts. Top with a favorite mayonnaise dressing.

1 Mix flour and seasonings. Dredge chicken breasts in seasoned flour.

2 Heat ¼ inch oil in skillet. When it is hot but not smoking, carefully add chicken. Fry over medium heat, turning once, until outside is crispy and no pink is visible when you cut into the chicken, 10–15 minutes, depending on the thickness of the chicken.

3 Let the chicken cool slightly. While it is cooling, divide the lettuce, mushrooms, celery, scallions, and olives between two plates. Cut the chicken into strips and arrange strips on top of salad. Serve with a mayonnaise dressing.

Avocado and Chicken Salad

Serves 4

- 🪶 1 lb. cooked chicken meat, in small chunks
- 🪶 2 ripe avocados
- 🪶 1 tbsp. lemon juice
- 🪶 4 tomatoes, skinned
- 🪶 2 scallions, chopped
- 🪶 2 tbsp. chopped fresh parsley
- 🪶 ½ cup cashew nuts, toasted

Garlic Vinaigrette

- 🪶 3 tbsp. groundnut oil
- 🪶 1 tbsp. white wine vinegar
- 🪶 1 tsp. Dijon-style mustard
- 🪶 1 clove garlic, minced
- 🪶 ½ tsp. superfine sugar
- 🪶 salt and freshly ground black pepper

Garnish

- 🪶 1 tbsp. chopped parsley

This is a quick, yet delicious, way of using up any left-over cooked chicken – a perfect summer lunch. Try ringing the changes with mango instead of avocado.

Stir-fry Chicken and Spinach Salad

Serves 4

- 🪶 6 oz. fresh young spinach leaves
- 🪶 6 small scallions, trimmed and sliced
- 🪶 2 tbsp. toasted filberts, chopped
- 🪶 2 small zucchini, thinly sliced
- 🪶 2 boneless half chicken breasts, skinned, approx. 5 oz. each
- 🪶 6 tbsp. light olive oil
- 🪶 1 small onion, finely chopped
- 🪶 1 clove garlic, finely chopped
- 🪶 2 tbsp. white wine vinegar
- 🪶 salt and freshly ground black pepper
- 🪶 1 tbsp. chopped fresh tarragon, or 1 tsp. dried

Garnish

- 🪶 1 small red bell pepper, seeded and diced

Russian Chicken and Potato Salad

1 Split the avocado in half, remove the pit and skin and cut into neat slices. Brush with the lemon juice to prevent discoloration.

2 Slice each tomato and arrange alternately with the avocado around the outer edge of a flat serving plate, as shown.

3 Mix the chicken with the scallions, parsley, and nuts. Whisk together the Garlic Vinaigrette ingredients. There should be enough to coat the chicken well.

4 Pile the mixture in the center of the plate. Brush any remaining dressing over the avocado and tomato slices. Garnish with a sprinkling of parsley.

This is a simple yet tasty salad topped with stir-fry chicken, onions, and garlic.

1 Rinse and lightly shake the spinach leaves. Tear into pieces and place in a bowl or on individual serving plates. Sprinkle on the scallions, filberts, and zucchini.

2 Cut the chicken into thin strips. Heat two thirds of the oil in a large, shallow pan and briskly stir-fry the chicken with the onion and garlic until just tender.

3 Stir in the remaining olive oil, wine vinegar, salt and pepper, and tarragon. Allow to cook for a further minute. Spoon the hot chicken and dressing over the salad ingredients.

4 Sprinkle with the diced sweet red pepper and serve immediately.

Serves 6

- 1½ lb. cooked, boned and skinned chicken
- 5 hard-cooked eggs
- ½ lb. baby or small red potatoes, boiled in their skins and thinly sliced
- 1½ cups cooked fresh or frozen peas, drained
- 2 large sour pickles, finely chopped
- scant 1 cup mayonnaise
- ½ cup sour cream
- 2 tsp. Worcestershire sauce
- salt and freshly ground black pepper
- 1 tbsp. chopped fresh dill
- black olives, halved
- 2 tbsp. capers

This real Russian salad is a traditional favorite, refined and Frenchified. It would make a delicious main course for a summer lunch or picnic.

1 Slice the chicken into ½ inch wide strips.

2 Finely chop two of the eggs. Place the chicken and chopped eggs in a large bowl, together with the potatoes, peas, and pickles.

3 In a smaller bowl, beat together the mayonnaise and the sour cream. Fold the Worcestershire sauce and half the dressing into the chicken mixture, seasoning to taste.

4 To serve in the Russian manner, mound the chicken salad in the center of a large serving dish. Slice the remaining eggs, and arrange the slices around the salad. Top each slice with a halved olive. Spoon the remaining dressing over the salad, and scatter the chopped dill and capers over the top. Chill for 30 minutes before serving.

Coronation Chicken

Serves 6

- 4 lb. chicken, cooked and removed from bones
- 1 tbsp. sunflower oil
- 1 small onion, finely chopped
- 2 tsp. curry powder
- 1 tsp. tomato paste
- ½ cup red wine
- 4 tbsp. water
- 1 bayleaf
- 2 slices lemon
- 4 tbsp. good quality apricot jam
- 1¼ cups low calorie mayonnaise
- 1¼ cups fromage frais or natural yogurt

Garnish

- paprika
- cucumber slices

This dish was developed by the Cordon Bleu Cookery School in London to celebrate the Queen's Coronation in 1953.

Tomato Salad with Chicken Liver Dressing

Serves 4

- 4 large tomatoes, peeled and thinly sliced
- 2 scallions, trimmed and chopped
- ½ cup sunflower oil
- 5 chicken livers, washed, trimmed, and chopped
- 1 clove garlic, finely chopped
- 1 tsp. wholegrain mustard
- 2 hardcooked eggs
- 4 tbsp. wine vinegar
- a few green peppercorns, crushed
- salt to taste

Garnish

Garnish

- 4 scallion curls (optional)
- snipped fresh chives

Vary this salad by adding thickly sliced mushrooms or sliced onions. The dressing is also good served with plain cooked chicken.

1 First prepare the tomatoes. Make an incision in the stem of each, and plunge in boiling water for 40 seconds. Drain and slip off the skins. Slice thinly onto the serving plate, and sprinkle with the chopped scallions. Chill.

1 Heat the oil, add the onion and cook for 3—4 minutes. Stir in the curry powder and cook for a further minute.

2 Add the purée, wine, water, bayleaf, and lemon slices. Simmer, uncovered, for about 10 minutes or until well reduced. Strain and cool completely.

3 Gradually beat the cooled sauce into the mayonnaise, then add the apricot jam and fromage frais or yogurt. Adjust the seasoning.

4 Lightly coat the chicken pieces with the mayonnaise. Pile onto a serving dish and garnish with a light dusting of paprika and thin slices of cucumber.

2 To make the dressing, heat 2 tbsp. of the oil. Sauté the livers with the chopped garlic until they just begin to brown.

3 Spoon the livers and garlic into a food processor or blender and blend together with the mustard, eggs, and vinegar. Gradually drizzle in the remaining oil.

4 Stir in the coarsely crushed peppercorns and season to taste. Spoon over the chilled tomatoes and serve immediately, garnished with a scallion curl and some snipped chives. Accompany with brown bread.

Hot and Spicy Bacon and Chicken Liver Salad

Serves 4

- ½ lb. chicken livers
- ½ tsp. ground coriander
- ¼ tsp. ground mace
- ¼ tsp. paprika
- 1 tbsp. all-purpose flour
- salt and freshly ground black pepper
- 2 scallions, chopped
- ⅓ cup chopped fresh parsley
- 1 tsp. grated lemon zest
- ½ lb. rindless bacon slices, diced
- 3 tbsp. olive oil
- salad of mixed leaves, to serve

Garnish

- lemon wedges

This is equally good as a light lunch or for supper, served with melba toast.

1 Rinse, drain and dry the chicken livers on paper towels. Trim any membranes from them, then halve or quarter each piece of liver. Sprinkle the coriander, mace, paprika, flour, and plenty of seasoning over the livers and mix well to coat all the pieces.

2 Mix the onion with the parsley and lemon zest, then set aside. Prepare the salad bases for serving the chicken livers.

3 Place the bacon in a cold pan and stir-fry over medium to high heat until the fat from the bacon runs. Continue to stir-fry until all the bacon pieces have become browned and are crisp. Use a slotted spoon to remove them from the pan and then drain the pieces on paper towels.

4 Add the olive oil to the fat remaining in the pan, heat it briefly, then add the chicken livers with all their seasonings. Stir-fry until firm, lightly browned and cooked – which should take about 5 minutes. Mix in the crispy bacon and the onion mixture.

5 Spoon the chicken livers onto the prepared salads.

6 To make melba toast, lightly toast medium-thick bread slices on both sides. Cut off the crusts and slice each piece through horizontally to give two very thin slices. Toast the uncooked sides of the bread well away from the heat source until lightly browned and slightly curled. Cool on a wire rack.

7 Garnish the dish with lemon wedges for their juice and serve it at once, with the melba toast.

Seafood Sauce with Chicken

Serves 4

- 3½ lb. chicken
- thinly pared rind of 1 lemon
- 1 small onion, thinly sliced
- 1 bayleaf
- 1¼ cups dry white wine
- 10 anchovy fillets
- 24 shrimps, shelled and shells reserved
- salt and freshly ground black pepper
- 1¼ cups low calorie mayonnaise
- juice of ½ lemon
- 2 tbsp. capers
- 7 oz. can tuna fish in brine

Garnish
- fresh basil sprigs

An unusual combination of fowl and fish which tastes exceptionally good. Serve with a crisp green salad and new potatoes.

1 Place the chicken in a large pan with the pared lemon rind, sliced onion, bayleaf, and white wine. Add sufficient water to come halfway up the chicken.

2 Chop 4 of the anchovy fillets and add them and the reserved shrimp shells to the pan, season, cover and bring to a boil, the simmer for about 1½ hours or until the chicken is tender.

3 Meanwhile, make the sauce. Blend together the mayonnaise, lemon juice, 1 tbsp. of the capers and the drained tuna fish. When smooth, season with salt and pepper to taste.

4 Remove the cooked chicken to a carving dish. Add sufficient of the strained cooking liquid to the tuna fish sauce to give a smooth, coating consistency.

5 Carve the cooked chicken while still warm and arrange on a flat platter. Spoon the prepared sauce over the top. Chill. Add to the chicken the shelled shrimp, remaining anchovy fillets, and capers. Garnish with fresh basil.

Minted Chicken and Melon Medley

Serves 4-6

- 6 half chicken breasts, boneless and skinned, each approximately 5 oz.
- 1¼ cups white grape juice
- salt and freshly ground black pepper
- ½ ripe rock melon (Charentais or Honeydew), seeded
- ½ ripe Ogen melon, seeded
- 1 cup seedless red grapes
- 1 cup feta cheese, cubed

Dressing

- 2 tbsp. light olive oil
- 1 tbsp. grape juice
- 1 tbsp. lemon juice
- 1 tbsp. fromage frais or light cream
- 1 tbsp. each freshly chopped mint and chives
- salt and freshly ground black pepper

Garnish

- fresh mint sprigs

We are fortunate to have a variety of melons available throughout the year. This fruit contrasts well with chicken, both in flavor and moistness. Serve this salad accompanied with crusty garlic brad for a light lunch.

1 Put the chicken, grape juice, and salt and pepper to taste in a pan. Bring to a boil, then simmer for 10 minutes, or until the chicken is tender. (Turn the chicken once during cooking.) Drain and cool.

2 Using a Parisienne cutter, scoop out the flesh of the melons to form neat balls. Alternatively, cut the flesh into 1 inch cubes. Place in a bowl with the halved grapes. Dice the chicken and add to the fruit, together with the cheese.

3 Shake the dressing ingredients together in a screw-top jar and gently fold into the salad. Chill for 30 minutes before serving, garnished with sprigs of mint.

Shrimp and Chicken Salad with Grapefruit, Mint, and Lemon Grass

Serves 6

- vegetable oil for deep frying
- about 40 shrimp chips
- 1 tbsp. unsalted peanuts
- 1 tbsp. sesame seeds
- 1 oz. dried shrimp, soaked in hot water for 30 minutes
- 2 oz. fresh pork sides
- ⅓ cup uncooked shrimp in the shells
- salt
- 1 medium cucumber, unpeeled, halved lengthwise, seeded and sliced thinly
- 1 large carrot, shredded
- 1 cup fresh beansprouts
- 1 oz. cooked chicken meat, cut into thin strips
- 1 tbsp. chopped fresh mint
- ½ tbsp. chopped lemon grass
- salt
- 1 large grapefruit, peeled, sectioned and cut crosswise into 1 inch pieces

Egg Pancakes

- 2 eggs
- ¼ tsp. soy sauce
- freshly ground black pepper
- vegetable oil
- 1 clove garlic, minced
- 1 fresh red chili, seeded and minced
- ½ tbsp. sugar
- ½ tbsp. fresh lime juice
- ½ tbsp. rice vinegar
- 1½ tbsp. soy sauce

Garnish

- cilantro sprigs

Served in hollowed grapefruit shells instead of a serving dish, this salad looks particularly attractive.

1 Heat about 2 inches oil to 350° in a wok. Add the chips 2–3 at a time and keep them immersed in the oil with a pair of chopsticks or slotted spoon until puffy. This should take about 10 seconds. Turn and cook for the same length of time. When finished, set aside.

2 Rub down the wok, return it to a moderate heat and cook the peanuts. Stir constantly until the peanuts are golden brown – about 5 minutes. Grind with a grinder of put between a couple of sheets of clean strong paper and grind with a rolling pin. Toast the sesame seeds in the same way for only 3 minutes. Grind lightly to a grainy texture.

3 To make the pancakes, beat the eggs, soya sauce and pepper together with ½ tsp. water in a bowl. Brush the bottom of a non-stick omelet pan with some oil and place over moderate heat until hot. Pour in half of the egg mixture and tilt the pan immediately to spread the mixture evenly over the bottom – the pancake should be paper-thin. Cook until the egg is set – this should not take more than 30 seconds. Turn and cook on the other side for about 15 seconds. Set aside. Repeat, using up the rest of the mixture and set aside.

4 Combine the garlic, chili, sugar, lime juice, vinegar, and soy sauce in a bowl. Stir to blend thoroughly. Set the dressing aside.

5 Drain the dried shrimp and pound or blend in a blender or processor until very fine. Set aside.

6 Cover the pork with water and bring to a boil over a high heat. Lower and boil for about 30 minutes or until the juices run clean when the meat is pierced with a knife. Run cold water over the pork and set aside.

7 Cook the raw shrimp in boiling water until just pink – about 2 minutes. Run cold water over them, drain, peel, de-vein, and cut lengthwise in halves. Shred the shrimp and set aside.

8 Sprinkle salt over the cucumber and carrot and let sit for 15 minutes. Run cold water over them and squeeze dry with your hands. It is imperative that the vegetables are bone dry to ensure their crunchiness.

9 Dip the beansprouts in salted boiling water for 30 seconds. Run cold water over them and drain.

10 Cut the egg pancakes into strips. Combine the egg pancake strips, dried shrimp, shredded shrimp, chicken, cucumber, carrot, beansprouts, mint, lemon grass, grapefruit, and sesame seeds. Mix well with your hands and pour over the dressing mixture.

11 Transfer to a serving dish or serve separately, and sprinkle the ground peanuts over it. Garnish with cilantro. Serve with shrimp chips on which guests place bite-sized portions of the salad.

Chicken Chantilly

Serves 4-6

- 2 tbsp. vegetable oil
- juice of ½ lemon
- 6 tbsp. white wine
- 3–4 pickling onions (or shallots), sliced
- 1 cup button mushrooms, sliced
- ⅔ cup chicken stock plus extra, if needed
- 1 tomato, peeled and deseeded
- 1 bayleaf
- scant 1 cup long grain rice
- 3½ lb. chicken, cooked
- 1¼ cups low calorie mayonnaise
- ⅔ cup fromage frais
- salt and freshly ground black pepper

Garnish

- 1 hard cooked egg (yolk sieved, egg white chopped)
- 1 lettuce heart
- strips of canned pimiento
- 2 tbsp. chopped fresh parsley

This is an ideal fork or buffet dish. It is very decorative and can be made in advance and assembled prior to serving.

1 Put half the oil, the lemon juice, wine, stock, mushrooms, onions, tomato, and bayleaf into a pan. Season well, bring to a boil, then simmer, covered, for 6–10 minutes.

2 Heat the remaining oil in a pan and stir-fry the rice until it begins to go opaque.

3 Strain off the liquor from the mushroom and onion, reserving the vegetables, and add enough boiling water or stock to make the quantity up to 2 cups. Pour this onto the rice, cover and cook until all the liquid is absorbed and the rice is just tender, about 20–25 minutes. Remove bayleaf, stir in the mushroom and onion and leave to cool.

Chinese Gooseberry and Chicken Salad with Strawberry Dressing

Serves 4

- 2 half chicken breasts, approx. 6 oz. each cooked and skinned
- 2 Chinese gooseberries, peeled and thinly sliced
- assorted salad leaves, washed

Dressing

- scant 1 cup strawberries, hulled
- 1 tsp. grated orange rind
- 4 tbsp. light olive oil
- 2 tbsp. red wine vinegar
- salt and freshly ground black pepper

Garnish

- 8 whole strawberries
- 1 tsp. green peppercorns, coarsely crushed

4 Arrange the rice mixture in a circle on a flat dish, leaving a hollow in the center.

5 Take the chicken meat off the bone and coarsely chop. Fold in the mayonnaise and fromage frais. Season to taste with salt and pepper. Pile on top of the rice pilaff.

6 Garnish the top of the chicken with crosswise strips of pimiento (sweet red pepper). Place the lettuce leaves in the center of the dish, and sprinkle with the sieved egg yolk. Mix the chopped egg white with the parsley and spoon a thin line around the edge of the rice. Serve chilled.

A delicious combination of strawberries and Chinese gooseberry harmonize well with the chicken to produce this colorful light salad.

1 Very thinly slice the cooked chicken breast and fan out the slices on four plates. Arrange the Chinese gooseberries on the chicken slices.

2 Arrange a few salad leaves at the point of the fanned chicken.

3 For the dressing, purée the strawberries. Whisk in the orange rind, olive oil, and wine vinegar. Season to taste with salt and pepper. Spoon over the chicken slices.

4 Garnish the salad with fresh strawberries and a sprinkling of coarsely crushed green peppercorns. Serve immediately.

Mediterranean Chicken Salad

Serves 6

- 6 oz. cooked chicken
- ¼ lb. cooked ham
- 1½ cups string or snap beans, lightly cooked
- 6 oz. new potatoes, cooked
- 4 plum or cherry tomatoes (yellow or red variety)
- ½ cucumber, peeled
- 12 black olives
- 1 tbsp. each chopped fresh basil, parsley, and chives
- 4 tbsp. olive oil
- 1 tbsp. white wine vinegar
- 1 tbsp. lemon juice
- dash dry mustard powder
- dash cayenne
- dash superfine sugar
- salt and freshly ground black pepper

Garnish

- 6 anchovies
- fresh herb sprigs

Fresh herbs make all the difference in this summer salad. For a change, substitute the ham with flaked tuna fish, and the basil with fresh tarragon.

1 Cut the chicken and ham into neat strips. Cut the beans into 1 inch lengths and the potatoes into small chunks. Place in a large bowl.

2 Halve or slice the tomatoes, depending on size. Cut the cucumber in half lengthwise, scoop out and discard the seeds, then cut the flesh into matchsticks. Add to the bowl.

3 Fold these ingredients together carefully, together with the freshly chopped herbs and olives.

4 In a screw top jar, shake together the olive oil, wine vinegar, lemon juice, mustard powder, cayenne, sugar, and seasonings until well blended. Pour over the chicken salad.

5 Spoon the salad into a glass serving dish. Garnish the top with fresh anchovies, and sprigs of fresh herbs. Chill for at least one hour before serving to allow the flavors to develop.

Smoked Chicken, Bacon and Shrimp Salad

Serves 4-5

- 6 oz. smoked chicken breast, cooked
- 1 cup shelled shrimp
- ½ cup thinly sliced button mushrooms
- 3 slices lean bacon, rinded
- selection of lettuce leaves

Dressing

- 6 tbsp. sunflower oil
- 2 tbsp. white wine vinegar
- dash dry mustard
- 1 shallot or ½ a small, sweet onion, finely chopped
- 4 tbsp. chopped fresh parsley
- salt and freshly ground black pepper

Garnish

- fresh chives

This salad makes the perfect starter, as it can be prepared well in advance and assembled at the last minute. Alternatively, serve this as a light lunch for two.

1 First make the dressing; combine the first five ingredients in a screw top jar and shake vigorously until well blended. Season with salt and pepper to taste.

2 Slice the chicken breast into thin strips. Place in a bowl together with the shrimp and mushrooms and pour over the dressing. Carefully fold the ingredients together. Cover and chill.

3 Broil the bacon until crisp. Crumble into a bowl.

4 Line four individual serving plates with an assortment of lettuce leaves. Drain the chicken mixture and spoon on top of the salad. Sprinkle with bacon, and garnish with fresh snipped chives.

Peach and Tarragon Sauce on Chicken

Serves 4

- 3 ripe peaches
- 1¼ cups dry white wine
- 2 strips lemon peel
- 1 tbsp. fresh tarragon, chopped or ½ tsp. dried
- salt and freshly ground black pepper
- 4 half chicken breasts, approx. 5 oz. each
- chicken stock
- ⅔ cup fromage frais (preferably low fat)

Garnish

- slices of skinned fresh peach (optional)
- fresh tarragon sprigs

Flavors of the summer enhance the chicken to make this an ideal meal to enjoy outdoors. Accompany it with a chilled stick or snap bean salad and new potatoes.

1 Make a nick in the stem end of each peach and plunge them into a bowl of boiling water for about 40 seconds. Lift out with slotted spoon and slip off the skins.

2 Halve the peaches and discard the pits. Chop the peach flesh roughly, and put in a pan with the wine, lemon peel, chopped tarragon and salt and pepper, to taste.

3 Simmer gently for 10 minutes; cool slightly, then blend until smooth.

4 Poach (or steam) the chicken breasts gently in the chicken stock until tender. Remove the skin and allow to cool.

5 Mix the cooled peach purée with the fromage frais. If the sauce is too thick, add a little liquid from poaching the chicken. Adjust seasoning.

6 Arrange the chicken breasts on a serving dish, spoon the peach sauce over the top and chill for an hour. To serve, garnish with slices of peach and sprigs of fresh tarragon.

3

Barbecued and Broiled Dishes

Fruity Chicken Kebabs with Curried Honey Glaze

Serves 4

- 4 large boneless half chicken breasts, skinned
- 8 slices streaky bacon, diced
- 16 dried apricot halves (non-soak variety)
- 2 firm bananas, cut into 1 inch slices
- 1 tbsp. lemon juice

Marinade

- 6 tbsp. clear honey
- 4 tbsp. light olive oil
- rind and juice 1 orange
- 2 cloves garlic, minced
- 1 tbsp. Worcestershire sauce
- 1 tsp. coriander seeds, crushed
- 1 tsp. curry powder
- salt

Kebabs are perfect for both a summer barbecue or a winter supper. They can be made well in advance and the ingredients can be varied to suit your own preference. Fruit and a curried honey marinade are delicious with chicken and help to keep it moist during cooking.

1 Shake all the marinade ingredients together in a screw top jar.

2 Cut the chicken into neat 1 inch cubes. Place in a bowl and pour over the marinade. Cover and keep in a refrigerator for 6 hours, or until required.

3 Stretch the bacon slices with the back of a knife. Cut each into half and form into rolls.

4 Alternately thread pieces of chicken, apricot halves, banana chunks, and bacon rolls onto skewers.

5 Brush with the remaining marinade and cook for 10–15 minutes under a pre-heated broiler turning and basting frequently, until the chicken is cooked and sizzling.

6 Serve warm with crusty bread and salad.

Note: If you are using bamboo skewers, soak these in water for 30 minutes beforehand to prevent them from burning.

Lemon and Pepper Chicken Thighs

Serves 4

- 2 lemons
- 2 cloves garlic, finely chopped
- 2 tbsp. olive oil
- 2 tsp. coarsely ground black pepper
- salt
- 8 chicken thighs

This is a simple and quickly prepared chicken dish to cook over the barbecue.

1 With a zester, remove the peel from 1 lemon or grate finely so that only the yellow part is removed. Squeeze the juice from both lemons and put into a dish with the peel, garlic, oil, black pepper, and salt to season.

2 Add the chicken thighs, cover and marinate for at least 4–6 hours, preferably overnight.

3 Barbecue for 15–20 minutes, turning halfway through and brushing with the marinade.

Lime Chicken Breasts

Serves 4

- 🍋 4 skinned boneless half chicken breasts, trimmed of fat, halved and tendon cut to flatten
- 🍋 5 tbsp. olive oil
- 🍋 freshly squeezed juice of 3 limes
- 🍋 4 cloves garlic, minced
- 🍋 3 tbsp. chopped fresh cilantro
- 🍋 ½ tsp. each salt and freshly ground black pepper

Sweet bell peppers lend extra pizazz to this simple dish. Throw some red and yellow peppers on the barbecue while you're at it, or serve with a sweet pepper chutney and noodles tossed in melted butter flavored with lime juice.

1 Pound chicken between layer of wax paper to flatten more. In a bowl, combine olive oil, lime juice, garlic, 2 tbsp. cilantro, salt and pepper. Pour over chicken and marinate at least 1 hour.

2 Broil or barbecue the chicken breasts 2 minutes on each side. Remove to a platter. Sprinkle with remaining cilantro and serve immediately.

Jerk Mon's Chicken

Serves 4-6

- 4 tsp. allspice berries, crushed in mortar and pestle, or 1 tsp. ground allspice
- 6 cloves garlic, minced
- 2 tbsp. peeled and chopped fresh ginger root
- 2 tbsp. dark brown sugar
- 3 tbsp. yellow mustard
- 1 tsp. ground cinnamon
- 3 tbsp. chopped chiles
- hot pepper sauce, to taste
- ½ cup olive oil
- 2 scallions, sliced
- ¼ cup cider vinegar
- 2 tbsp. lime juice
- salt and freshly ground black pepper
- 3–3½ lb. chicken, jointed, or 6 large whole legs or 4 large breasts

**This jerk dish incorporates a classic rub – a combination of spices, brown sugar and chiles that is applied to the chicken to enliven the dish.
To make the dish extremely hot use *habañero* or Scotch Bonnet chiles.**

1 Purée the chiles in a blender or food processor. Add the allspice, garlic, ginger, sugar, mustard, cinnamon, hot pepper sauce, olive oil, scallion, vinegar, and lime juice and blend until the mixture is a smooth paste. Add salt and pepper to taste and blend again.

2 Cut the chicken legs and thighs apart. Cut breasts in half crosswise, leaving the wings attached. Gently lift the skin up from the chicken, exposing the meat, and rub the paste underneath. Then rub into the outside of the skin. Cover with plastic wrap and refrigerate for 2 hours.

3 Barbecue or broil the chicken for about 40 minutes at low heat, turning once, until the skin is dark brown and crusty.

4 To cook on a covered barbecue, place the coals on one side and the chicken on the other. Cover and cook for 40–50 minutes.

5 To cook in the oven, preheat it to 350°F. Bake the chicken for 50 minutes then transfer to the broiler and cook for 2–3 minutes on each side until the skin is dark brown and crusty.

Garlic Chicken on a Stick

Serves 6

- 6 half chicken breasts, skinned and boned
- 6 cloves garlic, minced
- salt and freshly ground black pepper, to taste
- freshly squeezed juice of 2 lemons
- 8 tbsp. olive oil
- 6 tbsp. very finely chopped fresh parsley

A handy tip is to soak the wooden skewers in lemon juice for 30 minutes before using them. This gives a lovely tangy flavor to the chicken and helps to prevent the sticks from burning under the broiler.

1 Cut the chicken into 1 inch pieces and place in a shallow dish.

2 In a small bowl, mix together the garlic, salt and freshly ground black pepper, lemon juice, and olive oil. Pour the marinade over the chicken pieces, stir, cover and marinate for 2–4 hours in the refrigerator, turning and rearranging them occasionally.

3 Spread the chopped parsley out on a plate. Divide the chicken pieces into six equal portions and thread on to six wooden skewers. Roll each skewer in the chopped parsley to coat evenly.

4 Arrange the chicken skewers on an oiled broiler rack and cook under a preheated broiler for 5–10 minutes or until the chicken is golden on the outside and cooked through. Turn and rearrange the skewers, basting them with the remaining marinade during cooking for an even more delicious result.

Oregano Chicken

Serves 6-8

- 6–8 chicken portions
- ⅓ cup olive oil
- ⅓ cup dry white wine
- 2 tbsp. dried marjoram
- salt and freshly ground black pepper, to taste
- 2 cloves garlic, minced

This simple, tasty dish is perfect for the barbecue on a hot summer's day, or broiled for a fast snack.

1 Arrange the chicken portions in a large, shallow dish.

2 In a small bowl, combine the oil, wine, marjoram, salt and freshly ground black pepper, and the garlic. Mix well. Spread the marinade over the chicken portions, cover, and marinate for 2–3 hours, turning and re-arranging occasionally.

5 Place the chicken portions on an oiled broiler rack and cook under a preheated broiler for about 30 minutes or until the chicken is crisp and golden on the outside and cooked through, turning and rearranging several times during cooking. Serve warm or cold.

Avocado and Nectarine Salsa with Barbecued Chicken

Serves 4

- 6 tbsp. olive oil
- 2 tbsp. fresh lime juice
- 3 tbsp. fresh orange juice
- 2 cloves garlic, minced
- 1 tbsp. chopped fresh cilantro
- ¼ tsp. hot pepper sauce
- 4 boneless half chicken breasts, with or without skin
- 1 tsp. freshly ground black pepper
- 6 oz. salsa of your choice

Avocado Salsa (makes about 1 lb.)

- 2 large, ripe avocados, peeled, pitted, and diced
- 3 tbsp. fresh lime juice
- 1 tbsp. olive oil
- 3 oz. red onion, minced
- scant ½ cup diced sweet red bell pepper
- 3 jalapeño chiles, minced, some seeds included
- ¼ cup seeded and chopped tomato (about 1 large)
- 1 tbsp. chopped fresh cilantro
- 2 cloves garlic, minced
- salt and pepper to taste

Nectarine Salsa (makes about 6 oz.)

- 3 ripe nectarines, peeled, pitted, and chopped
- 4 tbsp. finely chopped scallions
- 1 jalapeño or serrano chili, finely chopped, some seeds included
- scant ½ cup finely chopped sweet red bell pepper
- 2 tbsp. chopped fresh basil
- 2 tbsp. fresh lime juice
- ¼ tsp. chili powder
- salt and pepper to taste

In this recipe, chicken breasts are marinated in a simple, spicy, citrus marinade, then barbecued over hot coals. It is a dish that tastes excellent hot or cold. It's also delicious cut into chunks and served on a green salad, topped with salsa – Avocado Salsa and Nectarine Salsa are particularly good.

1 Make the marinade by mixing together all the ingredients except the chicken, the salsa and the black pepper. Put the chicken in a plastic or glass bowl and pour the marinade over it. Turn the chicken breasts so they are thoroughly coated, then let marinate, refrigerated, for at least 6 hours or overnight. Turn the chicken 2 or 3 times while it is marinating.

2 About an hour before serving time, start the fire in the barbecue. When the flames have died, and the coals are glowing and covered with white ash (about 40 minutes), sprinkle the chicken breasts with black pepper and put them on the greased grid over the coals. Barbecue, turning once, until the chicken is cooked through, about 12 minutes, depending on the thickness of the meat and the distance from the coals.

3 To make the Avocado Salsa: mix the avocado chunks with the lime juice and olive oil, then stir in the remaining ingredients. Taste and adjust the seasoning.

4 To make the Nectarine Salsa: with a fork, mash about 2 tbsp. of the chopped nectarine. Stir in the rest of the nectarine and the remaining ingredients. Let sit for about 15 minutes, then taste and adjust the seasoning.

5 Serve the salsa on top of the chicken or on the side.

Greek Yogurt Chicken

Serves 6

- 6 chicken legs
- 3 cloves garlic, minced
- salt and freshly ground black pepper, to taste
- 1 tsp. paprika
- 1 tsp. ground cinnamon
- dash cayenne pepper
- freshly squeezed juice of 1 lemon
- 8 tbsp. olive oil
- 8 tbsp. Greek yogurt

Garnish

- lemon wedges, to serve

Chicken legs are used in this recipe, but other chicken portions work equally well. The yogurt is used not only for flavor but also to tenderize the meat, making it more succulent and juicy.

1 Place the chicken legs in a large, shallow dish. In a medium-sized bowl, combine the garlic, salt and freshly ground black pepper, paprika, cinnamon, cayenne pepper, lemon juice, oil, and Greek yogurt.

2 Pour the marinade over the chicken legs, stirring and turning them to coat evenly. Cover and leave to marinate in the refrigerator for 2–3 hours or overnight.

3 Season the chicken legs again with plenty of salt and freshly ground black pepper. Place the chicken legs on an oiled broiler rack under a preheated broiler and cook for 20–40 minutes or until crisp and golden on the outside and cooked through, turning frequently during cooking. Serve with lemon wedges.

Carib-Orient Chicken

Serves 4

- 3½ lb. chicken, cut into 2 inch pieces
- ½ cup soy sauce
- 2 tbsp. brown sugar
- 2 cloves garlic, minced
- 1 tbsp. grated fresh ginger root
- 3 tbsp. white wine

This is a simple, tasty dish that comes from Guyana.

1 Wash the chicken pieces and put them in a bowl.

2 Combine the remaining ingredients in a large saucepan and stir over a medium heat until the sugar has dissolved. Leave to cool.

3 Pour the sauce over the chicken and let marinate for 5 hours.

4 Broil the chicken pieces until they are tender and serve.

Yakitori Chicken Skewers

Serves 2 or 4

- 1 clove garlic, chopped
- 1 inch piece fresh ginger, peeled and chopped
- 5 tbsp. soy sauce
- 4 tbsp. mirin (sweet rice wine) or dry sherry
- 4 tbsp. sake
- 2 tbsp. sugar
- 1 lb. boned and skinned chicken meat, cut into 1 inch cubes
- 6–8 scallions, trimmed and cut into 1 inch lengths
- 1½ cups mushrooms, halved

Garnish

- ½ cucumber, sliced,

Mirin is available from Japanese food shops – dry sherry can be used as a substitute. Serve these skewers as a starter, or with plain boiled rice as a main course. Chicken livers are sometimes included in Yakitori.

1 In a bowl mix together the garlic, ginger, soy sauce, rice wine, sake, and sugar. Stir in the chicken cubes. Cover with plastic wrap and let marinate for 1–2 hours.

2 Thread the chicken onto bamboo skewers 6–8 inches long, alternating with the scallions and mushrooms. Brush with the marinade and arrange under a preheated broiler.

3 Cook for 8–10 minutes, basting frequently with the marinade, and turning the skewers several times, until the chicken is cooked through.

4 Serve immediately, garnished with cucumber slices.
Note: Soak bamboo skewers for 30 minutes before using to prevent them from burning.

Chicken Koftas

Serves 6-8

- 3 half chicken breasts, skinned, boned and finely minced
- 1 cup fresh white bread crumbs
- ½ cup pine nuts, ground
- 3 tbsp. finely chopped fresh parsley
- ½ tsp. ground turmeric
- 1 egg, beaten
- salt and freshly ground black pepper, to taste
- flour, for dredging
- olive, oil, for shallow frying
- freshly squeezed juice of 1 lemon

The chicken mixture in this recipe could be formed into ball or sausage shapes around skewers and broiled or barbecued to be served warm or cold, sprinkled with lemon juice.

1 Place the chicken in a mixing bowl and add the bread crumbs, pine nuts, parsley, and turmeric. Mix well to combine.

2 Add the beaten egg to the chicken mixture and season with salt and freshly ground black pepper. With slightly damp hands, shape the chicken mixture into balls the size of walnuts and place on a baking sheet lined with wax paper.

3 Sprinkle the balls lightly with flour. Heat the oil in a deep non-stick skillet and fry the chicken balls, a few at a time, for about 5–8 minutes or until crisp and cooked through, turning them to ensure they cook evenly. Transfer the cooked chicken balls to an ovenproof dish and place in a low oven to keep warm while the remaining batches are cooked. Serve warm or cold, sprinkled with lemon juice.

Chicken Tikka with Mint Chutney

Serves 4

- 1½ lb. boneless chicken, cubed

Marinade

- 1 small onion, finely chopped
- 2 cloves garlic, finely chopped
- ½ tsp. salt
- 1 tsp. hot chili powder
- 1 tsp. paprika
- ½ tsp. ground ginger, or 1 tsp. grated fresh ginger
- ½ tsp. ground cumin
- 1 tbsp. lemon juice
- ⅔ cup natural yogurt

Mint Chutney

- 3 tbsp. mint sauce
- 2 tsp. chili powder
- 1 small onion, finely chopped
- 1 tsp. salt

Garnish

- onion rings
- lemon wedges

These chicken tikka kebabs can be barbecued or broiled, and are accompanied with a mint relish. Serve them as a starter to an Indian meal or as a main course. They are good cold, in a lunch box or picnic.

1 Grind the onions and garlic to a paste with the salt. Blend in the spices and lemon juice and mix into the yogurt.

2 Stir in the chicken, cover and leave to marinate for 1–2 hours.

3 Thread the chicken onto skewers and cook under a hot broiler for 10–15 minutes or until the chicken is tender.

4 Meanwhile, make the Mint Chutney by mixing together all the ingredients. Chill.

5 Garnish the tikka kebabs with onion rings and lemon wedges, and serve with the Mint Chutney and chapatis or naan bread.

Tandoori-style Chicken

Serves 4-6

- 6 boned chicken thighs, skinned
- 6 chicken drumsticks
- 2 tbsp. lemon juice
- ⅔ cup natural yogurt
- 2 cloves garlic, minced
- 1 tbsp. tomato paste
- 1 tsp. ground cardamom
- 1 tsp. chili powder
- 1 tsp. ground cumin
- 1 tsp. paprika
- ½ tsp. grated fresh ginger

Yogurt Dressing

- ⅔ cup natural yogurt
- 1 tbsp. chopped scallions
- 1 tbsp. chopped fresh mint
- 1 tbsp. chopped fresh cilantro
- salt and freshly ground black pepper

This dish can be prepared a day or two in advance and left, chilled, to marinate. It is equally good hot or cold, and served simply with a tomato and onion salad and freshly baked naan bread. The chicken can also be barbecued.

1 Make several small incisions with the tip of sharp knife in the chicken. Brush with the lemon juice.

2 In a large bowl, blend together the yogurt, garlic, tomato paste, ground spices, and grated ginger. Add the chicken and mix well. Cover and let marinate for at least 6 hours, but preferably overnight.

3 To make the yogurt dressing, mix all the ingredients thoroughly, season and chill until needed.

4 Line an ovenproof dish with foil, place chicken and marinade in the dish, cover and bake for 45 minutes at 350°F or until the chicken is tender. Remove foil and cook for a further 15 minutes or until browned. Accompany with the yogurt dressing.

Chicken Saté

Serves 4

- 2 tbsp. coconut cream or natural yogurt
- 1 clove garlic, minced
- 1 tsp. chili powder
- 1 tsp. ground cumin
- 1 tsp. ground coriander
- 1 tbsp. lemon juice
- ½ lb. chicken, cubed

Dipping Sauce

- 3 tbsp. roasted peanuts or 3 tbsp. crunchy peanut butter
- 1 red chili pepper, finely chopped
- 1 clove garlic, minced
- 1 tbsp. finely chopped mint
- 1 tbsp. lime or lemon juice
- 3 tbsp. light soy sauce mixed with 1 tsp. anchovy extract
- 2 tbsp. sesame oil
- ½ cup thin coconut milk

1 Combine the coconut cream or yogurt with the garlic, chili powder, cumin, coriander, and lemon juice. Marinate the chicken pieces in the mixture for at least 4 hours, turning frequently.

2 Make the dipping sauce by mixing and pounding all the dipping sauce ingredients together except for the coconut milk. A rough paste should result. Stir in the coconut milk.

3 When the chicken is ready, thread it on to four skewers. Place on the barbecue or under a preheated high broiler and cook until well done, basting frequently with the marinade and turning.

4 Heat the dipping sauce and serve separately.

Spicy Barbecued Chicken with German-style Potato Salad

Serves 6-8

- 4–5 lb. chicken portions
- 2 tbsp. olive oil
- 2 tbsp. ground cumin
- 1½ tsp. turmeric
- 1 tsp. hot or mild paprika or chili powder

Garnish

- fresh cilantro leaves

German-style Potato Salad

- 2 lb. waxy potatoes, cooked, peeled and cut into ½ inch cubes
- 2 German-style dill pickles, diced
- 2 tbsp. vegetable oil
- 1 onion, finely chopped
- 1 clove garlic, finely chopped
- 1 stalk celery, strings removed, finely chopped
- salt
- freshly ground black pepper
- 1 tbsp. light brown sugar
- 1 tbsp. German mustard
- ¼ cup red or white wine vinegar

Garnish

- chopped fresh cilantro or parsley

Barbecued foods are very popular in Israel and the variety is amazing. Try this easy recipe using chicken. Serve with lots of hot potato salad.

1 Rub the chicken portions with olive oil. Arrange on a baking sheet and sprinkle spices equally over both sides. Leave to stand while preparing a barbecue.

2 Position barbecue rack about 5 inches above preheated coals. Arrange any legs and thighs on rack and cook 10 minutes. Add any breast portions to rack and cook 7–10 minutes longer. Raise rack if chicken browns too quickly.

3 Turn chicken portions over and cook breasts 7–10 minutes longer and legs and thighs 12–15 minutes longer, or until juices run clear when chicken is pierced with a knife or skewer.

4 In a large bowl, place warm potatoes. Add diced dill pickles. Set aside.

5 In a medium skillet, over medium-high heat, heat oil. Add onion, garlic, and celery and cook until onion just begins to soften 2–3 minutes. Add salt and pepper to taste. Stir in sugar, mustard, and vinegar until well blended.

6 Pour over potato-pickle mixture; toss gently to mix. Spoon into serving bowl and sprinkle with parsley for garnish. (If you like, drizzle with additional oil.)

7 Arrange chicken on a large serving platter and garnish with cilantro or parsley leaves.

BELOW: *Spicy Barbecued Chicken*

ABOVE: *German-style Potato Salad*

Red-legged Chicken

Serves 4

- 8 chicken drumsticks
- 1 large sweet red bell pepper
- 1 tsp. paprika
- ½ tsp. cayenne
- 1 tbsp. lemon juice
- 2 tbsp. sunflower oil
- 1 clove garlic, minced
- salt

Delicious hot or cold and perfect for a picnic, prepare these drumsticks well in advance for barbecuing, broiling, or roasting.

1 With a sharp knife, make 2 or 3 small incisions in each chicken drumstick.

2 Put the sweet pepper under a hot broiler and cook until the skin is blistered all over. Place in a plastic bag and leave to sweat for 10 minutes.

3 Remove the skin and seeds from the pepper, chop roughly, and blend in a food processor or blender, together with the remaining ingredients.

4 Pour the purée into a shallow dish, add the chicken drumsticks and turn them thoroughly in the purée to coat evenly. Cover and chill for at least 4 hours or preferably overnight, to allow the flavors to be absorbed.

5 Either cook the drumsticks over hot barbecue coals, broiler, or transfer to a roasting pan and cook in a preheated oven at 400°F for 35–40 minutes or until tender.

Garlic Chicken with Garlic Sauce

Serves 4-6

- 3 x 1½ lb. Rock Cornish game hens, halved and flattened, or 6–8 chicken pieces
- 1 tbsp. paprika
- salt and freshly ground pepper
- 4 tbsp. Garlic Sauce
- 3 cloves garlic, minced
- 3 tbsp. olive oil
- 2–4 tbsp. lemon juice
- fresh watercress
- lemon quarters

Garlic Sauce (makes 1 cup)

- 45 cloves garlic, skinned and minced
- ⅔ cup olive oil
- juice of 1 lemon

This treatment is particularly good with whole Rock Cornish game hens, split in half, flattened with a mallet and rubbed with paprika, then submerged in the marinade. It can also be made with tender chicken pieces.

1 Rub the flattened chicken halves or pieces with the paprika and salt and pepper, making sure that the spices are well distributed.

2 Make the Garlic Sauce: put the garlic into a processor bowl and blend briefly to chop the garlic finely. Then slowly add the oil in a stream with the motor running. You should have a smooth purée. Finally, add the lemon juice. Blend briefly and transfer to a bowl. (The sauce can be kept refrigerated for 2 weeks or more, or frozen.)

3 In a small bowl, whisk together the 4 tbsp. Garlic Sauce, the olive oil and 2 tbsp. lemon juice.

4 Pour the marinade over the chicken, turning the pieces in it. If necessary, add a little more oil. Cover and chill overnight.

5 Barbecue the hen halves or chicken pieces over hot coals, which are whitening with ash. Turn 3 or 4 times, until browned and lightly charred on the outside, but succulent within. This will take 20–40 minutes, depending on the size of the pieces. Check by inserting a skewer into a meaty part; the juice should run clear. (Alternatively, cook under a preheated oven broiler, turning occasionally, until done.)

6 Serve the chicken hot, on a bed of watercress with lemon quarters for squeezing over, and Garlic Sauce.

ABOVE: *Garlic Sauce*

RIGHT: *Garlic Chicken*

Skewered Chicken

Serves 6

- ⅓ cup olive oil
- 1 tbsp. freshly squeezed lemon juice
- 1 tbsp. wine vinegar
- ¼ cup dry red wine
- 2 cloves garlic, minced
- 1 tsp. dried mint
- 4 half chicken breasts, skinned, boned and cut into 1 inch cubes
- ½ lb. chicken livers, cut into small pieces
- 2 green bell peppers, seeded and cut into chunks
- 12 medium-sized mushrooms, cleaned
- 12 cherry tomatoes

Yogurt, Cucumber and Garlic Dip

- 1 lb. natural yogurt
- ½ cucumber
- 3 cloves garlic, minced
- 2 tbsp. chopped fresh mint
- 2 tbsp. olive oil
- 1 tbsp. white wine vinegar
- salt, to taste

Garnish

- chopped fresh mint

This classic Greek dish should be served with plenty of garlicky dip and warm pitta bread.

1 In a small bowl, combine the oil, lemon juice, wine vinegar, red wine, garlic, and mint. Mix well.

2 Arrange the chicken breasts and chicken livers in a shallow dish. Pour the marinade over the chicken and stir to coat. Cover and marinate in the refrigerator for 2–3 hours, stirring occasionally.

3 Thread the chicken, chicken livers, peppers, mushrooms, and cherry tomatoes alternately and equally on to six metal skewers. Brush with any remaining marinade and place on an oiled broiler rack under a preheated broiler. Cook for 20–25 minutes or until crisp and cooked through, turning and rearranging during cooking.

4 To make the dip, place the yogurt in a medium-sized bowl. Peel and grate the cucumber, squeezing a little at a time in the palm of your hand to remove the excess water. Stir the cucumber into the yogurt.

5 Stir in the garlic, fresh mint, olive oil, and vinegar and season with salt, to taste. Çover and chill in the refrigerator until required. Just before serving, garnish with chopped fresh mint.

Indo-Caribbean Chicken Pelau with Coconut

Serves 6

- 1 onion, chopped
- 2 cloves garlic
- 1 tbsp. chopped fresh chives
- 1 tbsp. chopped fresh thyme
- 2 stalks celery with leaves, chopped
- 4 tbsp. water
- fresh coconut meat from ½ coconut chopped
- liquid from fresh coconut
- 1 lb. can pigeon peas, drained
- 1 fresh chili
- 1 tsp. salt
- freshly ground black pepper
- 2 tbsp. vegetable oil
- 2 tbsp. sugar
- 3½ lb. chicken, chopped
- generous 1 cup uncooked rice, washed and drained
- 1¼ cups water

This traditional dish from Trinidad of chicken with rice and pigeon peas uses fresh coconut. When you buy the coconut, shake it to make sure it has liquid inside – this is a sign that the coconut is fresh.

1 Grind the onion, garlic, chives, thyme, and celery with 4 tbsp. water in a blender or food processor. Empty the mixture into a large saucepan.

2 To open the coconut, puncture two of its "eyes" – the darker dots on one end – with a small, sharp knife or an ice pick. Drain all the liquid from the coconut, then tap the whole surface of the shell lightly with a hammer. Now give the shell a sharp blow with the hammer. This will open the coconut, and the meat will now come away from the shell.

3 To make the coconut milk grate the coconut meat. Measure the coconut and stir in an equal amount of hot, but not boiling, water. Cover a bowl with a piece of cheesecloth, and strain the coconut through the cloth, pressing down hard on the coconut with a wooden spoon to extract as much liquid as possible. If you measure 1¼ cups of coconut meat to 1¼ cups of water, you should produce 1¼ cups of coconut milk.

4 Add the coconut milk to the pan, together with the pigeon peas and hot pepper. Cook over a low heat for 15 minutes, then season with the salt and freshly ground black pepper to taste.

5 Heat the oil in a flameproof casserole. Add the sugar and heat until it begins to caramelize.

6 Add the raw chicken to the casserole, and cook for 15 minutes until it has browned. Stir in the pigeon pea mixture, rice and 1¼ cups of water. Bring to a boil, reduce the heat, cover, and simmer for 20 minutes or until the rice and chicken are cooked. Discard the hot pepper before serving.

White Wine Braised Chicken with Tomato and Rice Stuffing

Serves 6

- scant 1 cup cooked brown rice
- 3 oz. garlic sausage, chopped
- 1 tbsp. chopped fresh parsley
- 3 tomatoes, skinned, seeded and chopped
- salt and freshly ground black pepper
- 2 egg yolks
- 3½ lb. chicken
- 1 sweet red bell pepper
- 2 tbsp. olive oil
- 1 shallot or small sweet onion, finely chopped
- 1 cup large cup mushrooms, thickly sliced
- 1¼ cups chicken stock
- 2 tsp. cornstarch
- 3 tbsp. light cream
- 2 tsp. chopped fresh basil (½ tsp. dried)

Nutty brown rice is used in the stuffing to make this a perfect dinner party recipe. Serve the sauce separately for those who want to control the flow of calories.

1 Prepare the stuffing by mixing together the rice, garlic sausage, parsley, tomatoes, and 1 egg yolk. Season with salt and pepper. Spoon inside the neck end of the chicken and fold the flap of skin over (securing with a small metal skewer if necessary).

2 Place the sweet red pepper under a hot broiler, and turn until it is blistered all over. Put in a plastic bag and leave to sweat for 10 minutes. The skin can then easily be removed. Discard the seeds and thickly slice the flesh.

3 Heat the oil in a large flameproof casserole, add the chicken and cook over a moderate heat, turning until golden brown all over. Lift out and set aside; add the shallots or onion and mushrooms to the pan and cook for a few minutes until softened.

4 Return the chicken to the casserole, add the sliced sweet pepper and pour over the wine and stock. Cover and cook in the oven at 350°F for 1 hour 20 minutes, or until tender.

5 Lift the chicken out onto a serving dish and remove the skewer if necessary. Using a slotted spoon, arrange the mushrooms and peppers around the chicken, and keep warm.

6 Stir the basil into the pan and simmer on the hob for 5 minutes. Beat the remaining egg yolk, cornstarch and cream together and stir into the pan. Heat gently until the sauce thickens.

7 Joint or carve the chicken and accompany each serving with a spoonful of stuffing. Serve the sauce separately.

Pistachio Roasted Chicken

Serves 6-8

- ¼ cup olive oil
- 2 onions, finely chopped
- generous 1 cup long-grain rice
- 4 large tomatoes, skinned, seeded and chopped
- 2 cups shelled pistachio nuts, roughly chopped
- ⅔ cup seedless raisins
- dash ground cinnamon
- salt and freshly ground black pepper, to taste
- 2¼ cups boiling water
- 3 tbsp. very finely chopped fresh parsley
- 3½ lb. chicken, without giblets
- ¼ cup dry white wine

This is a variation of one of Greece's most popular dishes. The chicken should be cut up into pieces and served with the stuffing separately.

1 Preheat the oven to 450°F. Heat half of the olive oil in a large, heavy skillet and sauté the onion for about 5 minutes or until softened.

2 Add the rice to the skillet and continue to cook for a further 3 minutes or until the rice begins to brown, stirring occasionally. Add half of the tomatoes, the pistachios, raisins, cinnamon, salt and freshly ground black pepper and ¾ cup boiling water. Simmer for about 10 minutes or until the liquid is mostly absorbed and the rice is almost cooked, stirring continuously. Remove from the heat and stir in the parsley.

3 Spoon the rice mixture into the cavity of the chicken without packing it too firmly. Place the chicken in a roasting pan and spoon any remaining rice mixture around the outside. Season the chicken with salt and freshly ground black pepper.

4 Scatter the remaining chopped tomatoes around the chicken and pour 1½ cups boiling water and the wine into the pan. Reduce the oven temperature to 350°F (the chicken skin is seared and made crispy before the oven adjusts to the lower heat). Drizzle the remaining olive oil over the chicken and roast for about 1½ hours or until the chicken is cooked through and the rice, inside and outside of the chicken, is tender. Baste the chicken during cooking and add a little extra water if necessary. Let sit for 10 minutes before serving it with the stuffing.

Mexican Rice Chicken

Serves 6

- 🌶 3½–4 lb. chicken
- 🌶 2 medium onions, chopped finely
- 🌶 2 cloves garlic, chopped
- 🌶 2 serrano chiles, chopped (fresh or canned)
- 🌶 1 lb. peeled and seeded tomatoes or
  1 can tomatoes
- 🌶 ¼ cup olive oil
- 🌶 1 lb. long-grain rice
- 🌶 ¼ tsp. whole cumin seed
- 🌶 ¼ tsp. saffron
- 🌶 3¾ cups chicken stock
- 🌶 salt and pepper
- 🌶 generous 1 cup peas, fresh or frozen

This recipe adds chicken to authentic spicy Mexican or Spanish Rice.

1 Cut the chicken into serving pieces. Fry until golden; drain and set aside. In the same oil, fry the chopped or sliced onion together with the garlic. Drain, and add to the chicken, together with the tomatoes, stock and spices. Bring to a boil; simmer for about half an hour.

2 Meanwhile, still in the same oil – adding a little more if necessary – fry the rice until it is golden, stirring frequently. Add the rice to the chicken; mix well; bring back to a boil, stirring frequently.

3 When the rice has absorbed all the visible liquid (10–20 minutes), add the peas; stir briefly; then cover tightly and simmer over a very low heat for another 20 minutes or so.

Stuffed Sweet Peppers

Serves 4

- 4 even-sized sweet bell peppers
- 2 tbsp. sunflower oil
- 1 small onion, finely chopped
- generous ½ cup long grain rice
- ½ cup button mushrooms, chopped
- 2¼ cups chicken stock
- 4 tbsp. tomato paste
- 2 tbsp. chopped fresh basil
- salt and freshly ground black pepper
- 4–6 chicken livers, chopped
- 2 tbsp. pinenuts, toasted
- 2 tbsp. finely grated Parmesan cheese

Garnish

- fresh basil leaves

When buying the sweet bell peppers, choose squat round peppers which still stand upright. Choose green, red, yellow or orange peppers, or even a mixture. Serve accompanied with a bowl of hot fresh tomato sauce.

1 Cut the tops off the peppers and remove the cores and seeds. Put the peppers in a bowl, cover with boiling water and let sit for 5 minutes. Drain thoroughly and set aside.

2 Heat half the oil in a large pan and sauté the onion until softened. Stir in the rice and mushrooms and cook for a further minute; add the stock, bring to a boil and simmer, covered, for 15 minutes, until the rice is just tender and the stock absorbed.

3 Stir in the tomato paste and the freshly chopped basil. Season to taste.

4 Heat the remaining oil and sauté the chicken livers until lightly browned. Stir into the rice with the pinenuts.

5 Spoon the rice mixture into the peppers and sprinkle them with the cheese.

6 Arrange the peppers in an ovenproof dish. Pour a little water into the dish (just enough to cover its base) and cook for 35 minutes at 350°F or until the peppers are tender. Serve hot, garnished with fresh basil leaves.

Chicken Pilaf

Serves 6-8

- ½ cup butter
- 2 lb. chicken breasts, skinned, boned and cut into bite-sized pieces
- salt and freshly ground black pepper, to taste
- dash ground cinnamon
- dash ground allspice
- 2 onions, chopped
- 3 tbsp. tomato paste
- 2½ cups boiling water
- generous 1 cup long-grain rice
- ¼ cup butter

Garnish

- chopped fresh mint

The classic Greek way to finish preparing this dish, and also many others which use pasta or rice, is to brown some butter in a small pan and pour it over just before serving. It's an optional stage in this version, and if you are particularly worried about your fat intake you might like to leave it out.

1 Melt the butter in a large, heavy-based saucepan and sauté the chicken pieces for 5–10 minutes or until lightly browned, turning during cooking. Add the salt and freshly ground black pepper, cinnamon, and allspice, and stir well.

2 Add the onions to the saucepan and continue to cook until softened. Stir in the tomato paste and boiling water. Cover and cook for 20 minutes; then add the rice. Cover and continue to simmer for a further 20–25 minutes or until the chicken is cooked through and the rice is tender.

3 Remove the cover for the final 10 minutes of the cooking time to allow the liquid to be absorbed. Melt the butter in a small skillet and cook until browned. Turn the pilaf out on to a warm serving platter and pour the browned butter over the top. Sprinkle with chopped fresh mint to serve.

Caribbean Chicken and Rice Stew

Serves 6

- 🦐 1 clove garlic, chopped
- 🦐 ½ tsp. dried marjoram
- 🦐 ½ tsp. salt
- 🦐 3½ lb. chicken, cut into 8 pieces
- 🦐 4 tbsp. butter or margarine
- 🦐 1 small onion, finely chopped
- 🦐 generous 1 cup chopped green peppers
- 🦐 4 ripe tomatoes, skinned and chopped
- 🦐 1¾ cups uncooked long-grain white rice
- 🦐 4½ pt. chicken stock
- 🦐 freshly ground black pepper
- 🦐 1 lb. frozen peas
- 🦐 ½ cup freshly grated Parmesan cheese
- 🦐 1 fresh chili, chopped

This tasty chicken stew comes from Puerto Rico.

1 Mix the garlic, marjoram, and salt together in a large bowl. Add the chicken pieces, and mix them well together. Heat the butter or margarine in a saucepan, and brown the chicken pieces. Transfer them to a plate.

2 Add the onion and green peppers to the pan, and cook until soft.

3 Add the tomatoes and browned chicken pieces, coating them well with the onion, peppers, and tomato mixture. Reduce the heat and simmer for 30 minutes, or until the chicken is cooked.

4 Remove the chicken to a plate and leave to cool a little.

5 Remove the bones, and cut the flesh into 2 inch pieces.

6 Meanwhile, add the rice, stock and freshly ground black pepper to the onion, peppers and tomato mixture, and bring to a boil. Reduce the heat, cover, and simmer for 20 minutes or until the rice is cooked.

7 Stir in the peas, Parmesan, and chili. Mix well, then add the chicken. Cover and simmer for 2 more minutes, then serve.

Chicken Fried Rice with Chili Fish Sauce

Serves 4

- 3 tbsp. peanut or corn oil
- 7 oz. boneless skinned chicken breasts, cut lengthwise into ½ inch thick slices
- 1 tbsp. chopped garlic
- 1 medium-sized onion, sliced
- 2 eggs
- 1¼ lb. cooked rice
- 1 tomato, cut into 8 wedges
- 1 scallion, chopped
- 2 tsp. white soy sauce
- 1 tsp. commercially available fish sauce
- 1 tsp. sugar
- 1 tsp. ground white pepper

Chili Fish Sauce

- ¼ cup fish sauce
- 10 fresh small green chiles, sliced into small circles
- 1 tsp sliced shallot
- ¼ tsp. sugar
- 1 tbsp. lime or lemon juice

One of the basic standard Thai dishes, this always tastes best with rice from the day before – and is easier to cook if the rice has been chilled in the refrigerator for a while. In place of chicken, pork or shrimp are also commonly used. The spicy sauce is found on all Thai tables and is used to add both spiciness and saltiness to dishes.

1 Heat the oil in a wok or pan, add the chicken and garlic and mix well over the heat for 1 minute. Add the onion and cook for 1 minute, break in the eggs, mix very well and then stir in the rice and the rest of the ingredients. Stir well. Cook for 2 minutes and serve immediately.

2 To make the Chili Fish Sauce, mix all the ingredients together well.

3 Serve the fried rice accompanied by cucumber slices, whole scallions and the Chili Fish Sauce.

Chicken Rice

Serves 4

- 11 oz. boneless chicken breasts
- 5 cups water
- 3 cilantro roots
- 2 tsp. salt
- generous 1 cup rice, rinsed
- 10 cloves garlic, chopped
- ½ oz. ginger, sliced and crushed
- 3 tbsp. peanut or corn oil
- 5 inch piece of cucumber, cut into ¼ inch slices

Garnish

- ¼ oz. cilantro leaves

Khao Man Sauce

- 5 fresh small green chiles, chopped
- 2 tbsp. pickled soy beans
- ½ tbsp. chopped fresh ginger
- ½ tbsp. white vinegar
- 1 tsp. sugar
- 1 tsp. black soy sauce
- ¼ tsp. chopped garlic

A very popular day-time dish, and Chinese in origin, its special feature is that the rice is cooked in chicken broth. The chicken pieces are always arranged on top of the mound of rice.

1 Boil the water in a pan, add the chicken with the cilantro root and salt, and cook until the chicken is soft, about 15 minutes.

2 Remove the meat with a slotted spoon and put to one side. Strain the cooking liquid, put 3¾ cups back in the pan and add the rice, garlic, ginger, and oil.

3 Bring back to a boil and cook, covered, until the rice is tender but not soft, about 15–18 minutes.

4 Place the rice on serving plates. Slice the chicken across into ½ inch pieces and place on top of the hot rice.

5 Arrange the cucumber slices around the sides and sprinkle with cilantro leaves.

6 Mix all the ingredients for the Khao Man Sauce together in a bowl and serve with the chicken and rice, and with the remaining cup of chicken broth if desired.

Chicken Risotto

Serves 4-6

- 1 lb. boneless chicken breast, skinned and cubed
- 2 tbsp. sunflower oil
- 1 onion, finely sliced
- 2 cloves garlic, minced
- 1 tsp. dried marjoram
- 9 oz. Arborio or long grain rice
- 1 tbsp. tomato paste
- 5 cups strong chicken stock
- splash dry white wine
- salt and freshly ground black pepper
- 6 tomatoes, skinned, seeded and chopped
- 10 pitted black olives, halved

Garnish

- ½ cup grated Parmesan cheese

A true Italian risotto uses Arborio rice, which contributes to the characteristic creamy texture. If you prefer a slightly wetter risotto, add a little more stock (or wine!).

1 Heat the oil in a large pan, and cook the onion and garlic over a gentle heat until softened. Add the chicken and cook until golden brown.

2 Add the marjoram and rice and cook for a further minute, stirring well. Blend in the tomato paste, stock, and wine. Season to taste and stir well.

3 Cook over a gentle heat for 25–30 minutes or until the liquid is absorbed, but the rice still has a nutty bite to it.

4 Lightly fork in the tomatoes, olives, and chopped parsley or basil. Heat through for a further 2 minutes. Serve, sprinkled with the Parmesan cheese.

Cilantro Chicken with Pilau Rice

Serves 4

- 1 tbsp. sunflower oil
- 8 chicken thighs
- 1 large onion, sliced
- 1 tsp. paprika
- 1 tsp. ground cumin
- 1 tsp. turmeric
- ½ tsp. dried thyme
- freshly ground black pepper
- 1¼ cups well flavored chicken stock
- 1 oz. pitted black olives
- 2 tbsp. finely chopped fresh cilantro
- squeeze lemon juice

Pilau Rice

- 2 tbsp. vegetable oil
- ½ cup whole blanched almonds, toasted
- 1 small onion, finely diced
- ⅓ cup golden raisins
- scant 2 cups long grain rice
- 3 cups boiling water
- ½ tsp. salt

Fresh cilantro has a unique, pungent flavor.

1 Heat the oil in a large pan and fry the chicken until an even, rich brown. Transfer to a plate.

2 Add the onion to the remaining oil and cook until softened and golden. Stir in the paprika, cumin, and turmeric and cook for a further minute. Add the thyme, black pepper, and stock and bring to a boil.

3 Return the chicken to the pan, skin side down. Cover and simmer for 1–1¼ hours or until the chicken is tender.

4 Remove the chicken with a slotted spoon to a heated serving dish and keep warm.

5 Reduce the sauce by rapidly boiling until it thickens. Stir in the olives, cilantro, and lemon juice. Season to taste and pour over the chicken.

6 For the rice, heat the oil in a large pan and cook the onion until softened but not colored. Add the toasted almonds, sultanas, and rice, and cook for a further minute, stirring thoroughly.

7 Add the boiling water and salt. Bring to a boil, then cover and reduce the heat to a simmer. Cook for 15 minutes, or until all the water has been absorbed and the rice is tender, but still firm. Fork the rice lightly and serve with the chicken.

Crispy Chicken Chow Mein

Serves 4

- 4 Chinese dried mushrooms
- 3 boneless half chicken breasts, skinned
- 2 tbsp. cornstarch
- salt
- ¾ lb. Chinese egg noodles
- 4 tbsp. oil
- 1 tbsp. sesame oil
- 1 oz. fresh ginger root, peeled and cut into short thin strips
- 4 stalks celery, cut into thin, 1 inch strips
- 1 bunch scallions, shredded diagonally
- 4 tbsp. soy sauce
- ⅔ cup chicken stock
- 4 tbsp. dry sherry

Chow mein is a Chinese dish consisting of egg noodles mixed with other ingredients. This combination of textures, which results from frying the noodles before topping them with sauce, is delicious.

1 Place the dried mushrooms in a mug or small bowl. Add just enough boiling water to cover them, then put a small saucer over them and weight it down to keep the mushrooms submerged. Let sit for 20 minutes. Drain the mushrooms, reserving the liquid, then discard any woody stems and slice the caps.

2 Cut the chicken into thin slices, then into fine strips. Place in a bowl or plastic bag and coat with the cornstarch, adding a little salt. Cook the noodles in a large pan of boiling salted water for 3 minutes. Drain well, then place the noodles in a large skillet and lightly pat them into a flat cake; set aside.

3 Heat half the oil and the sesame oil in a wok or large saucepan. Add the chicken and stir-fry until the strips are lightly browned. Add the ginger root, celery, scallions and mushrooms, and cook for a further 3 minutes. Stir in the mushrooms and add the reserved soaking liquid from the dried mushrooms. Pour in the soy sauce and stock and bring to a boil, stirring all the time. Leave to simmer while you cook the noodles.

4 Slide the noodles from the skillet onto a plate. Heat the remaining oil in the skillet, then slide the noodles into it. Cook until crisp and golden underneath. Use a large pancake turner to turn the cake of noodles over. Alternatively, slide the noodle cake out onto a plate, then invert it back into the skillet. Cook the second side until crisp and golden.

5 Slide the noodles out onto a large platter, then pour the chicken mixture over the top. Serve at once. Diners break off portions of noodles with chopsticks or a spoon and fork, taking some of the chicken mixture with the portion. The noodles soon soften in the sauce, so they must be eaten promptly.

Blushing Chicken Livers

Serves 4

- 1 lb. chicken livers
- 1 tbsp. butter
- 1 tbsp. vegetable oil
- 1 large onion, diced
- 1 clove garlic, minced
- ½ tsp. hot chili powder
- 3 tomatoes, peeled, seeded and sliced
- ¼ cup button mushrooms, sliced
- 2 tbsp. tomato paste
- ½ cup red wine or Marsala
- ½ tsp. chopped fresh thyme
- dash ground bayleaves
- 1 tsp. Worcestershire sauce
- salt and freshly ground black pepper
- ⅔ cup fromage frais

Garnish

- chopped fresh parsley

Here the chicken livers are quickly cooked in a spicy tomato sauce. They are good served with jacket potatoes, creamed potatoes or noodles and a green salad.

1 Rinse the chicken livers and pat dry on paper towels.

2 Heat the butter and oil in a saucepan. Sauté the onions and garlic until lightly browned and softened.

3 Sprinkle in the chili powder and stir in the chicken livers. Cook for 4 minutes.

4 Add the tomatoes and mushrooms and cook for a further minute. Then stir in the tomato paste, red wine or Marsala, herbs, and Worcestershire sauce. Simmer, uncovered, for 4 minutes. The liquid will reduce a little.

5 Season to taste and stir in the fromage frais.

6 Serve immediately, garnished liberally with chopped parsley.

Chicken Cacciatore

Serves 4

- 4 chicken joints, skinned, approx. 7 oz. each
- ¼ cup all-purpose flour, seasoned
- 3 tbsp. vegetable oil
- 8 pickling onions or shallots, peeled
- 1 clove garlic, finely chopped
- 1 cup button mushrooms, halved
- 1 sweet green bell pepper, seeded and cut into strips
- 2 cups chopped tomatoes and juices (canned)
- ⅔ cup dry white wine
- 2 tbsp. tomato paste
- 2 tbsp. red wine vinegar
- 1 tsp. chopped fresh basil
- 1 tsp. chopped fresh marjoram
- salt and freshly ground black pepper, to taste
- ½ cup black olives

Garnish

- chopped basil or parsley

This Italian dish is delicious simply served on a bed of spaghetti.

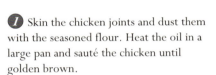

1 Skin the chicken joints and dust them with the seasoned flour. Heat the oil in a large pan and sauté the chicken until golden brown.

2 Add the onions and garlic and cook for a further 4 minutes. Sprinkle in any remaining flour, the mushrooms and green pepper and gradually blend in the tomatoes and juice. Stir in the remaining ingredients apart from the olives. Check seasoning.

3 Cover and simmer for 20–30 minutes or until chicken is tender. Ten minutes before the end, stir in the olives.

4 Serve, garnished with freshly chopped basil or parsley.

Bokari Pilaf

Serves 4

- 1 lb. chicken livers
- 4 tbsp. vegetable oil
- 2 onions, peeled and diced
- 1 clove garlic, minced
- 2 carrots, grated
- scant 2 cups basmati or long-grain rice
- salt and freshly ground pepper
- ½ tsp. turmeric
- 2½ cups chicken stock
- ⅛ cup canned tomatoes or 3 tomatoes, skinned

Garnish

- 2 tbsp. chopped fresh parsley

Chicken livers are generally sold frozen and are economical, nutritious and require little preparation. Always cut away any green tinged liver, which will taste bitter, and wash and dry them well. This recipe is very quick to prepare and good served with cucumber rings.

1 Trim and dice chicken livers.

2 Heat the oil in a large pan and fry the livers until golden brown.

3 Add the onions, garlic, and carrots to the chicken livers and turn with a spoon for about 2 minutes.

4 Add the washed rice, seasoning, turmeric, and stock. Cover and cook for 20 minutes. Remove the lid and stir gently. Add the chopped tomatoes and cook for a further 5–10 minutes until the rice is tender.

5 Sprinkle with chopped parsley and turn into a heated serving dish.

Blue Chicken

Serves 4

- 2 tbsp. olive oil
- 1 clove garlic, minced
- 1 sweet red bell pepper, seeded and diced
- 1 lb. boneless chicken, skinned and diced
- salt and freshly ground black pepper
- 2 cups small button mushrooms
- 4 tbsp. dry white wine
- ⅔ cup light cream
- ½ lb. blue cheese, cut into small pieces

Garnish

- 2 scallions, finely chopped
- 2 tbsp. chopped fresh parsley

Blue cheese makes a rich sauce for chicken or turkey. Serve large quantities of plain fresh pasta noodles to balance the full flavor of the sauce. Here Danish blue is used but any other blue cheese may be substituted – dolcelatte, for example, or tangy gorgonzola for a really powerful flavor.

1 Heat the oil in a large skillet. Add the garlic, sweet red pepper, and chicken with some seasoning – go easy on the salt at this stage as the blue cheese can make the sauce quite salty. Cook, stirring often, for about 20 minutes, or until the diced chicken is lightly browned and cooked.

2 Add the mushrooms and cook for 2 minutes, then pour in the wine and bring to a boil. Turn the heat to the lowest setting and make sure the mixture has stopped boiling before pouring in the cream and stirring in the cheese. Stir over low heat until the cheese has melted. Do not allow the sauce to simmer or it will curdle.

3 When the cheese has melted, taste the sauce, then pour it over the pasta and sprinkle with the scallions and parsley. Serve at once.

Tropical Stir-fry

Serves 4

- 1 small onion, finely chopped
- 4 tbsp. sunflower oil
- 1 clove garlic, minced
- 2 boneless half chicken breasts, approx. 6 oz. each, skinned and cut into thin strips
- 1 tbsp. sunflower seeds
- scant ⅓ cup salted cashew nuts
- ½ ripe, pink skinned mango, pitted and thinly sliced
- 2 Chinese gooseberries, peeled and sliced
- 4 kumquats, halved
- salt and freshly ground black pepper
- 2 tbsp. flaked coconut

The wonderful thing about stir-fry recipes is that any number or combination of ingredients can be used. Serve with plain boiled rice.

1 Stir-fry the onion in half the oil for 3 minutes. Add the remaining oil, garlic and the chicken and stir-fry briskly until the chicken is evenly colored and almost tender.

2 Add the sunflower seeds and cashew nuts and stir-fry for a further minute. Add the mango, Chinese gooseberries, kumquats, and salt and pepper to taste. Stir-fry for a further 2–3 minutes.

3 Sprinkle with flaked coconut and serve immediately.

Paprika Chicken

Serves 4

- 3½ lb. chicken
- 2 tbsp. vegetable oil
- 2 medium onions, peeled and thinly sliced
- 2 tsp. paprika
- ⅓ cup dry white wine
- 1 lb. tomatoes, seeded and chopped or 14 oz. can tomatoes
- 1 tbsp. tomato paste
- 2 whole canned pimentos, roughly chopped
- bouquet garni
- salt
- 4 tbsp. natural yogurt

Garnish

- 1 tbsp. chopped fresh parsley

Paprika chicken uses, as the name implies, the subtle, milder dried red pepper – never to be confused or substituted for hotter members of the family like cayenne or chili. Serve this warming dish with noodles or pasta shells.

Speedy Chicken Livers with Pasta

Serves 4

- 9 oz. dried pasta shapes
- 2 tbsp. vegetable oil
- 9 oz. chicken livers, cleaned and sliced
- 2 oz. lean bacon, rinded and chopped
- 2 small zucchini, sliced
- 4 scallions, trimmed and sliced
- 1 cup button mushrooms, sliced
- 1 small sweet red bell pepper, halved and cut into strips

- 2 tbsp. red currant jelly
- ⅔ cup dry white wine or chicken stock
- 2 tsp. chopped fresh sage
- 4 tbsp. natural yogurt or fromage frais
- salt and freshly ground black pepper

Garnish

- freshly chopped parsley

This chicken liver dish makes an all-in-one lunch or supper dish. If you do not wish to use pasta, serve the chicken livers on a bed of boiled brown rice.

1 Cook the pasta in boiling salted water until *al dente* (cooked but firm when bitten).

2 Meanwhile heat the oil in a pan and add the chicken livers and bacon and stir-fry for 1 minute. Add the zucchini, scallions, mushrooms, and peppers, and cook for a further 2 minutes.

1 Joint the chicken into 8 pieces, and remove the skin where possible.

2 Heat the oil in a large pan and sauté the chicken until browned. Remove and set aside. Add the onions to the pan and cook until softened.

3 Sprinkle in the paprika and cook for a further minute. Blend in the wine.

4 Return the chicken pieces to the pan together with the tomatoes, paste, pimentos, bouquet garni and salt to taste. Cover and simmer for 45 minutes.

5 Transfer the chicken to a serving dish to keep warm. Rub the contents of the pan through a sieve. Return to rinsed pan and reheat. Season to taste.

6 Swirl in the yogurt and pour over the chicken pieces. Sprinkle with the chopped parsley. Serve immediately.

3 Stir in the red currant jelly, wine or stock, sage, and salt and pepper. Cover and simmer for 4–5 minutes.

4 Drain the pasta. Fold the chicken livers together with the yogurt or fromage frais.

5 Sprinkle thickly with chopped parsley and serve immediately.

Mushroom, Spinach and Chicken Lasagne

Serves 6

- 10–12 oz. green pre-cooked lasagne, approximately 12 sheets
- ½ cup freshly grated Parmesan cheese

Chicken and Nutmeg Sauce

- 1 tbsp. sunflower oil
- 1 small onion, finely chopped
- 1 lb. uncooked chicken meat, cut into ½ inch cubes
- ½ cup butter
- 1 cup all-purpose flour
- 3¾ cups semi-skimmed milk
- ½ tsp. freshly grated nutmeg
- salt and freshly ground black pepper

Mushroom and Spinach Mixture

- 1 tbsp. sunflower oil
- 1 onion, finely chopped
- 3 cloves garlic, minced
- 3 cups flat mushrooms, finely chopped
- ¾ lb. fresh spinach, washed
- salt and freshly ground black pepper

A tasty lasagne, accompanied with a crisp salad and crusty brown bread makes for easy and informal entertaining. Prepare the lasagne in advance and chill until you are ready to cook it.

1 To make the chicken sauce, heat the oil in a pan and cook the onion gently until softened. Add the diced chicken and stir-fry until the chicken is firm and cooked through.

2 In another saucepan, melt the butter. Add the flour and cook, stirring, for one minute. Remove from the heat and slowly blend in the milk, beating to a smooth sauce between each addition. Season with the nutmeg, salt and pepper.

3 Put a third of the sauce into a bowl and reserve. Add the chicken and onion mixture to the remaining sauce. Place a layer of damp wax paper on the surface of both sauces to prevent a skin forming.

4 For the mushroom and spinach mixture, heat the oil and cook the onion and garlic gently until softened. Add the mushrooms and cook gently for 10 minutes or until any liquid has evaporated.

5 Cook the spinach briefly in a large covered saucepan until it has softened and reduced in volume. There is no need to add any water. Drain, squeeze out any excess liquid and then chop finely. Add to the mushroom mixture and season to taste.

6 Lightly oil a deep rectangular ovenproof dish approx. 12 x 7 inches. Line the bottom and sides of the dish with some of the pasta and then layer with half the chicken sauce, pasta, spinach and mushroom sauce, more pasta, the remaining chicken sauce, pasta and the plain sauce.

7 Sprinkle with the grated Parmesan and cook for 45–50 minutes at 375°F or until bubbling and golden brown on top.

Won Tons of Chicken with Vegetables

Makes about 50 – Serves 4

- 4 boneless half chicken breasts, skinned
- ¼ tsp. five-spice powder
- 8 scallions, chopped
- 1 tsp. sesame oil
- 5 tbsp. soy sauce
- 1 clove garlic, minced
- 1 quantity won ton dough
- 1 egg, beaten
- 3 tbsp. oil
- 2 stalks celery, cut into fine 1 inch strips
- 1 red bell pepper, quartered, seeded and cut into thin strips
- ½ medium head Bok choy, shredded
- 3 tbsp. dry sherry

Won Ton Dough

- 3 cups all-purpose flour
- ½ cup cornstarch
- dash salt
- 1 egg, beaten
- ½ cup water

These chicken won tons are thicker than authentic won tons. This makes them easier to handle and quicker to fill – and they taste terrific! With the vegetables they make an ample complete meal; if they are served with a selection of other Chinese-style dishes, then they will yield far more portions.

1 Cut the chicken into 50 small pieces. Place them in a bowl and add the five-spice powder, 2 tbsp. of the scallions, sesame oil, 2 tbsp. of the soy sauce and the garlic. Mix well, cover and let marinate for 30 minutes.

2 Sift the flour, cornstarch and salt into a bowl, then make a well in the middle. Add the egg and pour in the water. Use a spoon to mix the egg and water into the flour. When the mixture binds together, scrape the spoon clean and use your hand to work the dough into a smooth ball, leaving the bowl free of mixture.

3 Place the dough on a clean surface and knead it thoroughly until it is very smooth. Cut the dough in half and wrap both portions in plastic wrap, then set aside for 15–30 minutes.

4 Dust the work surface and rolling pin lightly with cornstarch.

5 Cut the won ton dough in half. Roll out one portion into a 15 inch square. Cut the dough into 3 inch strips, then across into squares. Brush a square of dough with beaten egg. Place a piece of chicken in the middle of it, then fold the dough around the chicken and pinch it together well.

Continue filling the squares, placing them on a platter dusted with cornstarch as they are ready. Roll out the second portion of dough and make a further 25 won tons.

6 Grease a large covered dish with oil and set it to warm. Bring a large saucepan of water to a boil, then cook the won tons in batches, allowing 5 minutes after the water has come back to a boil. Drain, transfer to the dish and keep hot.

7 Stir-fry the vegetables while the won tons are cooking. Heat the oil in a large skillet. Add the celery and red pepper, and cook, stirring, for 5 minutes. Add the remaining scallions and cook for a further 2 minutes. Then add the Bok choy and cook for 3–5 minutes. Pour in the remaining soy sauce and sherry, and stir for 1 minute.

8 Arrange the vegetables and won tons together on a platter and serve at once.

Crispy Won Tons

Serves 4

- ½ quantity won tons as for Chicken Won Tons
- oil for deep frying

Sweet and Sour Sauce

- 2 tbsp. oil
- 1 tsp. sesame oil
- 1 onion, halved and thinly sliced
- 1 green bell pepper, halved, seeded and thinly sliced
- 1 carrot, cut into 1 inch strips
- 4 tbsp. tomato catsup
- 4 tbsp. soy sauce
- 1 tbsp. superfine sugar
- 2 tbsp. cider vinegar
- ⅔ cup dry sherry
- 1 tsp. cornstarch
- 2 canned pineapple rings, cut into small pieces

These won tons are made in the same way as the chicken won tons; however, they are deep-fried until crisp and served with a sweet and sour sauce. Offer them as a first course for a Chinese meal or serve them with plain boiled rice and a dish of stir-dried vegetables to make a delicious main course.

1 Make the won tons as for Chicken Won Tons but roll the dough again so it is paper thin. After filling pinch the dough to seal in the chicken, but leave the corners of the dough hanging free. Set them aside until the sauce is ready.

2 Heat the oil and sesame oil in a saucepan. Add the onion, green pepper, and carrot and cook for 5 minutes. Stir in the tomato catsup, soy sauce, sugar, cider vinegar, and sherry.

3 Bring to a boil, reduce the heat and simmer for 3 minutes.

4 Meanwhile, blend the cornstarch with 2 tbsp. cold water, then stir it into the sauce and bring to a boil, stirring all the time. Simmer for 2 minutes, then add the pineapple and set aside over low heat.

5 Heat the oil for deep frying to 375°F. Deep-fry the won tons a few at a time, until they are crisp and golden.

6 Drain them on paper towels. Place the won tons on a large flat dish or platter and spoon the sauce over them. Serve and eat at once.

Mushroom, Chicken and Tarragon Sauce

Serves 4

- 2–4 tbsp. melted butter
- 1 small onion, finely chopped
- 1 bayleaf
- 1 cup button mushrooms, sliced
- ¾ cup all-purpose flour
- 1¼ cups chicken stock
- ⅔ cup milk
- ½–¾ lb. boneless, skinned, cooked chicken, diced
- 2 tbsp. chopped tarragon
- salt and freshly ground black pepper
- ⅔ cup light cream

This is a simple sauce which goes well with any pasta. It may also be layered with lasagne, noodles or shapes in baked dishes. Turkey may be used instead of chicken.

1 Melt 2 tbsp. of the butter in a saucepan. Add the onion and bayleaf and cook, stirring occasionally, for 15 minutes, or until the onion is softened slightly but not browned. Add the mushrooms and continue to cook for 10–15 minutes, until they give up their juice and this evaporates completely, leaving the reduced vegetables and the butter.

2 Stir in the flour, then gradually pour in the stock and bring to a boil, stirring all the time. Stir in the milk, bring back to a boil, then add the chicken and tarragon with seasoning to taste. Reduce the heat, cover the pan and simmer gently for 10 minutes.

3 Stir in the cream and heat gently without boiling. If you like, beat in the remaining butter to enrich the sauce and make it rather special.

Noodles with Chicken, Vegetables and Gravy

Serves 4

- 11 oz. large flat rice noodles (sen yai)
- ½ cup peanut or corn oil
- 1 tsp. black soy sauce
- 2 tbsp. finely chopped garlic
- 7 oz. boneless skinned chicken breasts, cut lengthwise into ⅓ inch thick slices
- 2 tbsp. white soy sauce
- 2 tbsp. sugar
- 1 tsp. ground white pepper
- 1 cup chicken stock
- 1 lb. kale or broccoli, cut into ½ inch pieces
- 1 tbsp. cornstarch, mixed with a little water

If available, use the large flat noodles known as sen yai, rather than the thin variety.

1 Boil the noodles for 1 minute and drain well. Heat half the oil in a wok or pan, add the noodles, and fry lightly for 1 minute. Add the black soy sauce, fry lightly for another minute. Drain off the oil and transfer the noodles to a plate.

2 Heat the rest of the oil in the wok. Add the garlic and chicken, and fry lightly for 2 minutes. Stir in the white soy sauce, sugar, white pepper and then the chicken stock. Boil well for 3–5 minutes, add the kale, boil again for 1 minute and then add the cornstarch. Boil for 1 minute and pour over the noodles.

3 Serve accompanied by sliced fresh red chili in vinegar, fish sauce, sugar, and chili powder, in separate bowls.

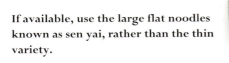

Ham and Chicken Lasagne

Serves 6-8

- ¾ lb. fresh lasagne verdi
- 2 cups diced cooked chicken
- 2 cups diced smoked ham
- 1 cup button mushrooms, chopped
- 6 scallions, chopped
- 2 tbsp. chopped fresh parsley
- 1 tbsp. chopped fresh sage
- salt and freshly ground black pepper
- 1¼ cup Monterey Jack or Colby cheese, finely crumbled
- paprika
- 1 cup fresh white bread crumbs

Béchamel Sauce

- 2 thick onion slices
- 2 bayleaves
- 2 mace blades
- 4 parsley sprigs
- 4¼ cups milk
- 6 tbsp. butter
- 1½ cups all-purpose flour
- salt and freshly ground white or black pepper

This is easy and delicious! Turkey may be used instead of chicken – a great way of using up the turkey roast. Add any leftover stuffing to the sauce too.

1 Cut the rolled-out pasta into large squares, about 5 inches, or rectangular sheets. Lower the pieces of pasta one at a time into a large saucepan of boiling salted water. Bring back to a boil and cook for 3 minutes. Drain and rinse under cold water. Lay the pasta on double-thick paper towels.

2 Butter a 12–15 x 8 inch ovenproof dish and set the oven at 350°F.

3 Place the onion, bayleaves, mace, and parsley in a saucepan. Add the milk and heat slowly until just boiling. Remove from the heat, cover and leave for 45 minutes.

4 Strain the milk into a jug or bowl. Wash the saucepan, then melt the butter and stir in the flour. Slowly pour in the milk, stirring all the time. Continue stirring until the sauce boils, then reduce the heat, if necessary, so that it just simmers. Cook for 3 minutes, stirring occasionally. Add seasoning to taste.

5 Set aside a third of the béchamel sauce. Lay a piece of dampened waxed paper directly on its surface to prevent a skin forming.

6 Mix the chicken, ham, mushrooms, scallions, parsley, and sage with the rest of the sauce. Taste for seasoning, then layer this sauce in the dish with the lasagne, ending with a layer of lasagne on top. Stir the cheese into the reserved sauce (it doesn't matter if the sauce is too cool for it to melt), then spread it over the top of the pasta.

7 Sprinkle with a little paprika and top with the bread crumbs. A mixture of crushed potato chips and a few finely chopped salted peanuts added to the bread crumbs makes a good topping.

8 Bake for 40–50 minutes, until the topping is crisp and golden and the lasagne layers are bubbling hot.

Oriental,
Hot
and Spicy

5

Caramelized Chicken Wings with an Orange Sauce

Serves 4

- 🦐 8 chicken wings
- 🦐 salt and pepper
- 🦐 2 tbsp. sesame oil
- 🦐 4 tbsp. clear honey
- 🦐 4 tbsp. vegetable oil
- 🦐 2 tbsp. superfine sugar
- 🦐 shredded rind and juice of 1 orange

This dish should have a slightly nutty, burnt flavor, but be careful not to burn the sugar.

1 Season the chicken wings with salt and pepper. Mix the sesame oil and honey and spread this over the wings.

2 Heat the oil in a heavy-based pan and cook the chicken wings for about 4 minutes on each side or until just done. Remove the pan and keep warm. Reserve the pan juices.

3 Add the sugar to the pan and heat without stirring until it caramelizes. Remove from the heat.

4 Add the orange juice and reserved pan juices. Stir over a low heat until a smooth sauce forms, adding a little water or orange juice if it becomes too thick. Add half the orange rind and continue to cook over a very low heat.

5 Place the chicken wings on to a warmed dish. Pour the caramel sauce over them and garnish with the leftover strips of orange.

Sweet and Sour Chicken

Serves 4-6

- 🦐 3¾ cups peanut or corn oil
- 🦐 1 lb. boneless skinned chicken breasts, cut across into ¼ inch slices
- 🦐 all-purpose flour for coating
- 🦐 1 medium-sized onion, sliced
- 🦐 1 medium-sized green bell pepper, sliced
- 🦐 ½ cup tomato catsup
- 🦐 1 cup tomato quarters
- 🦐 ½ cup diced pineapple
- 🦐 ½ cup chicken stock
- 🦐 2 tsp. white soya sauce
- 🦐 1 tsp. sugar
- 🦐 1 tsp. vinegar

This dish is popular with most people. It is not spicy but a spoonful of fish sauce will add zest.

1 Heat the oil in a wok or pan, coat the chicken lightly with flour and fry it until light brown, about 5 minutes. Remove and drain on paper towels.

2 Remove all the oil except for about ⅓ cup. Add the onion and pepper, cook for 1 minute, mix in the catsup, and then add the remaining ingredients. Stir-fry for 1 minute, add the chicken and continue to cook until the onion is tender, about 2 minutes.

3 Serve accompanied by rice and soy or fish sauce.

Lemon Chicken Chinese-style

Serves 4

- 1½ lb. boneless chicken breast, skinned
- 1 tbsp. cornstarch
- grated rind ½ lemon
- 2 tbsp. groundnut oil
- freshly ground black pepper

Sauce

- 4 tsp. cornstarch
- juice and rind 1 lemon
- 2 tbsp. clear honey
- 1 tsp. finely chopped stem ginger
- 2 tsp. stem ginger syrup
- 2 tsp. sesame oil
- 2 tsp. light soy sauce
- 1½ cups boiling chicken stock
- salt and freshly ground black pepper

Garnish

- 2 scallions, trimmed and finely chopped or snipped fresh chives
- julienne strips of lemon peel

The combination of lemon and chicken has been used in many good recipes and this one is no exception. It is quickly prepared and cooked and delicious accompanied with brown rice.

1 First make the sauce. In a pan blend the cornstarch with the lemon juice and rind to make a smooth paste. Stir in the honey, ginger, syrup and oil, and soy sauce. Pour on the boiling stock and bring to a boil, stirring, until thickened. Season to taste with salt and pepper. Simmer gently for 10 minutes.

2 Cut the chicken into 1 inch strips. Place in a bowl, and sprinkle with the cornstarch, lemon rind, and plenty of ground black pepper.

3 Heat the oil in a non-stick skillet. Add the chicken pieces and stir-fry for 10 minutes or until the chicken is golden brown and tender.

4 Transfer the chicken to a warm serving plate. Spoon over the lemon sauce and garnish with finely chopped scallions or chives and julienne of lemon peel. Serve immediately.

Gingered Chicken with Honey

Serves 4

- 2 tbsp. sunflower oil
- 4 half chicken breasts, skinned and part-boned, approx. 6 oz. each
- 2 inch fresh root ginger, peeled and cut into tiny matchsticks
- 2 medium onions, peeled and sliced
- 2 tsp. ground ginger
- 4 tbsp. light soy sauce
- 4 tbsp. dry sherry
- 2 tbsp. clear honey
- salt and freshly ground black pepper

Garnish

- 3 scallions, trimmed and finely chopped

This dish is very simply prepared and best accompanied with pilau rice.

1 Heat the oil in a pan and sauté the chicken pieces until golden.

2 Add the fresh ginger and onions to the oil and sauté until the onions soften. Stir in the ground ginger and cook for a further 2 minutes.

3 Return the chicken to the pan and cook for a minute more, then pour on the soy sauce, dry sherry and honey.

4 Cover with a tight-fitting lid and simmer for 30 minutes or until the chicken is tender.

5 Transfer the chicken and onions to a warm serving dish. Turn up the heat and boil the sauce to reduce it slightly. Season to taste.

6 Spoon the sauce over the chicken and garnish with a sprinkling of scallions. Serve hot.

Black Beans with Chicken

Serves 4

- 1 lb. chicken pieces (thighs, wings, breasts)
- 1 tbsp. soy sauce
- 1 tbsp. dry sherry or rice wine
- 1 tsp. sugar
- 2 tsp. cornstarch
- 2 tbsp. groundnut oil
- 1 tbsp. finely chopped fresh ginger
- 4 cloves garlic, finely chopped
- 2 tbsp. black beans, rinsed and coarsely chopped
- 2 scallions, finely chopped
- ½ sweet red bell pepper, cut into 1 inch squares
- ⅔ cup chicken stock

Black soy beans are available from good Chinese stores, and are sold either canned or packed in plastic bags (they need rinsing before use). These fermented, slightly salted beans partner the garlic and fresh ginger perfectly – to give a distinctive flavor, reminiscent of Chinese home cooking.

1 Chop the chicken pieces into 2 inch chunks. Mix the soy sauce, dry sherry, sugar, and cornstarch. Stir into the chicken pieces and leave to marinate for 1 hour.

2 Drain the chicken, discarding any marinade. Heat half the oil in a wok. Add the ginger and stir-fry briefly, then add the garlic and black beans. Cook for 2–3 minutes.

3 Add the chicken pieces and stir-fry for 4–5 minutes until they are browned. Add the scallions, red pepper and stock, reduce heat and simmer for 10 minutes.

4 Serve immediately with plain boiled rice.

Sesame Chicken

Serves 4

- 🦐 3 half chicken breasts, boneless and skinned, approx. 6 oz. each
- 🦐 2 tbsp. groundnut oil
- 🦐 1 tsp. dried chlli granules (or flakes)
- 🦐 1 tbsp. sesame seeds
- 🦐 2 stalks celery, trimmed and thinly sliced
- 🦐 1 tbsp. soy sauce
- 🦐 1 tbsp. dry sherry
- 🦐 1 tsp. cider vinegar
- 🦐 ½ tsp. salt
- 🦐 1 tsp. sesame oil

While sesame seeds have a very subtle flavor and add a crunchiness here in contrast to the tender chicken strips, sesame oil is much stronger so the little used in this recipe is to add flavor rather than for frying purposes. Serve this dish hot with some stir-fried vegetables. It is also delicious cold, as a salad.

1 Cut the chicken into fine diagonal shreds.

2 Heat 1 tbsp. of the oil in a wok or skillet and stir-fry the chicken and dried chili for 1 minute. Drain and transfer to paper towels.

3 Wipe the wok clean, heat the remaining groundnut oil and add the sesame seeds. Stir-fry for 1 minute or until golden brown.

4 Add the celery and stir-fry for a few seconds, before adding the remaining ingredients. Bring to a boil, return the chicken shreds and stir-fry for a further minute. Serve immediately.

Cashew Nuts and Chicken with Lemon Grass

Serves 4

- 🦐 vegetable oil
- 🦐 2 small dried chiles
- 🦐 1 clove garlic, chopped
- 🦐 1 lb. lean chicken, sliced
- 🦐 ½ tsp. sugar
- 🦐 1 tbsp. oyster sauce
- 🦐 1 tbsp. light soy sauce
- 🦐 3 tbsp. chicken stock or water
- 🦐 ½ cup roasted, unsalted cashew nuts
- 🦐 1 tbsp. lemon grass, chopped
- 🦐 2 shallots, cut in quarters

This Vietnamese recipe uses nuts and fresh herbs.

1 With a drop or two of oil, stir-fry the chiles until cooked evenly but not burnt. Set aside.

2 Stir-fry the garlic with a few more drops of oil until golden. Add the chicken slices, sugar and oyster and light soy sauce and stir-fry until the chicken is golden in color. Lower the heat and add the stock. Cook for a few more minutes, stirring occasionally.

3 When the chicken is thoroughly cooked, add the cashew nuts, lemon grass, shallots, and chiles, and stir several times, being careful not to break the chiles. Remove from the heat and serve.

Basil Fried Chicken

Serves 4

- 8 fresh green chiles, chopped lightly
- 8 cloves garlic, chopped lightly
- ¼ cup peanut or corn oil
- ¾ lb. boneless skinned minced chicken
- 2 fresh red chiles, quartered lengthwise
- 1 tbsp. oyster sauce
- ½ tsp. fish sauce
- ¼ tsp. black soy sauce
- ¾ oz. sweet basil leaves

1 Pound the green chili and garlic together with a mortar and pestle or in a blender.

2 Heat the oil in a wok or pan until hot, then add the chili-garlic mixture. Fry for 1 minute. Add the chicken and stir-fry for 1 minute; then add the red chili, oyster sauce, fish sauce, and soy sauce. Stir-fry for 2 minutes, mix the basil in well and serve immediately.

3 Serve accompanied by rice.

Ginger Fried Chicken

Serves 4

- ⅓ cup peanut or corn oil
- 1 tbsp. chopped garlic
- ¾ lb. boneless skinned chicken breasts, cut into ¼ inch thick slices
- 1 oz. wood fungus or fresh button mushrooms, sliced
- 4 scallions, cut into 1 inch pieces
- ½ cup onion, sliced
- 1 oz. fresh ginger, cut into small matchsticks
- 3 fresh red chiles, each sliced into 6 strips lengthwise
- 1 tbsp. white soy sauce
- 2 tbsp. brandy
- ½ tsp. sugar
- ¼ tsp. salt

1 Heat the oil in a work or pan, add the garlic and stir-fry, mixing well. Add the chicken, mix well for 1 minute, and then add the mushrooms. Stir for a minute and add all the rest of the ingredients. Stir-fry well until the chicken is cooked, about 8–10 minutes.

2 Serve accompanied by rice and soy or fish sauce.

Nasigoreng

Serves 4-6

- 1⅓ cups long grain rice
- 4 tbsp. groundnut oil
- 2 onions, finely chopped
- 1 clove garlic, finely chopped
- 1 fresh red chili, finely shredded
- 2 tomatoes, skinned, seeded and chopped
- 1½ cups cooked diced chicken
- 1 cup cooked shrimp, coarsely chopped
- salt and freshly ground black pepper
- 2 tbsp. chopped fresh cilantro

Omelet

- 1 tbsp. groundnut oil
- 3 scallions, finely chopped
- salt and freshly ground black pepper
- 2 tbsp. light soy sauce
- 4 eggs, beaten

Garnish

- paprika
- cucumber slices

This dish originates from Malaysia, and makes good use of any left-over cooked meat, fish, and vegetables. It is quick to prepare and makes the perfect informal fork supper dish.

1 Cook the rice until just tender. Drain thoroughly and spread out on a tray to cool.

2 Heat the oil in a large pan. Sauté the onions and garlic until softened and golden. Add the chili and cook for a further 2 minutes.

3 Stir in the tomatoes, chicken, and shrimp. Cook for 2 minutes, then add the rice. Stir-fry until the rice turns a light golden color. Season to taste. Stir in the fresh cilantro.

4 Mound the rice mixture onto a platter, cover and keep warm.

5 For the omelet, heat the oil in a large skillet. Add the scallions and cook until softened.

6 Season with salt and pepper and add the soy sauce. Cook for a further 2 minutes.

7 Stir the beaten eggs into the pan. Cook over a low heat until the omelet is set.

8 Carefully remove the omelet from the pan onto a chopping board. Loosely roll and shred it finely.

9 Arrange the shreds of omelet over the rice. Sprinkle with a light dusting of paprika and garnish with cucumber slices. Serve immediately, with extra soy sauce and a selection of salads and relishes.

Spiced Minced Chicken

Serves 6

- 1 lb. finely minced chicken
- ⅓ cup sliced shallots
- ¼ oz. cilantro leaves
- 4 tbsp. sticky rice, dry-fried for 8–10 minutes until brown and pounded finely
- 4 tbsp. lemon juice, or to taste
- 3 tbsp. fish sauce, or to taste
- 1 tbsp. chopped dried red chili, or to taste
- ½ tsp sugar

Garnish

- fresh mint leaves

One characteristic of the North-eastern Thailand version of this dish is the addition of uncooked sticky rice, roasted (in an oven or a dry wok) until golden and then pounded in a mortar. It adds a nutty flavor and gives the dish more body.

1 Cook the chicken in a non-stick pan over low heat for 10 minutes – do not add water or oil. When cooked, transfer to a bowl and mix in well all the remaining ingredients except the mint. Check the seasoning, and add more lemon juice, fish sauce or chili if necessary.

2 Sprinkle the mint over the top to garnish.

3 Serve accompanied by raw cabbage leaves, scallions, and raw string beans.

Bamboo Shoots and Mango with Chicken

Serves 4

- 1 lb. chicken, cubed
- 1 large carrot
- ½ red sweet bell pepper
- ½ green sweet bell pepper
- 1 cup bamboo shoots
- 1 large mango, just ripe and firm, cut into chunks
- 4 tbsp. vegetable oil

Marinade

- ½ tsp. baking soda
- 1 tbsp. sugar
- 1 egg white, lightly beaten
- 1 tbsp. cornstarch or potato flour

- salt
- water

Sauce

- 1 tsp. sugar
- 1 tbsp. light soy sauce
- 1 tbsp. oyster sauce
- 1 tbsp. sesame seed oil
- 1 tbsp. rice wine
- ½ tbsp. cornstarch or potato flour, mixed with a little water

1 Mix the marinade ingredients thoroughly and mix well with the chicken pieces. Let marinate for 30 minutes.

2 Trim and peel the carrot; cut into matchstick strips a little less than 1 inch long. Cut the peppers and bamboo shoots into strips to match the carrots. Cut the mango flesh into small, fairly thin pieces as neatly as possible.

3 Heat the oil in a wok and fry the chicken pieces for about 2 minutes. Remove from the oil and drain well. Add the carrot, peppers, mango, and bamboo shoots to the hot oil and fry in batches. Remove and drain thoroughly.

4 Rinse and dry the wok, add the chicken and vegetables and stir in all the sauce ingredients except the cornstarch. Stir-fry briefly and add the cornstarch to the sauce to thicken.

Sweet and Spicy Chicken

Serves 6

- 3½ lb. chicken, cut into 2 inch pieces
- 2 tbsp. olive oil
- 1 onion, finely chopped
- 2 scallions, finely chopped
- 2 cloves garlic, minced
- 1 fresh chili, chopped
- ½ tsp. brown sugar
- 1 tsp. thyme
- 1 tsp. basil
- 1 christophene, peeled, seeded, and chopped
- 1 eggplant, peeled and cubed
- ¼ lb. okra, trimmed and chopped
- 14 oz. can tomatoes, drained and chopped
- salt and freshly ground black pepper

The christophene used in this Caribbean dish is a pear-shaped tropical squash. It has a taste similar to zucchini or vegetable marrow.

1 Wash the chicken pieces.

2 Heat the oil in a large saucepan, and add the onion, scallions, and garlic. Cook over a low heat for 5 minutes.

3 Add the chicken pieces, and cook for 5 minutes to brown them.

4 Stir in the chili, sugar, herbs, and vegetables, and season to taste with salt and freshly ground black pepper. Pour in 1¼ cups cold water and bring to a boil, then lower the heat and, stirring occasionally, simmer uncovered for 1 hour or until the chicken and vegetables are cooked and the sauce has thickened.

5 Serve with fresh bread, baked yams, or boiled rice.

Indian-Jewish Chicken

Serves 4

- 3–3½ lb. chicken
- ½ cup vegetable oil
- salt
- freshly ground black pepper
- 1 onion, cut in half and thinly sliced
- 2 cloves garlic, finely chopped
- 2 bayleaves
- 1 cinnamon stick
- 4 whole cloves
- 4 cardamom pods
- 1 tbsp. curry powder or garam masala
- 1 tbsp. fresh ginger root, finely chopped or grated
- ¼ tsp. turmeric
- 1 cup chicken or vegetable stock or water

Garnish

- fresh parsley sprigs

This is a very aromatic dish, often served in the Bene Israel community of Bombay. It can be easily prepared and cooked overnight in a slow cooker or very low oven.

1 Rinse chicken in cold water and pat dry with paper towels. Remove legs and thighs from body and separate drumstick from thigh. Remove wing tips; remove breasts and wings from carcass and cut each breast into 2 pieces; upper breast portion can include wing. This gives you 8 pieces. (Wing tips and carcass can be used for soup.)

2 Preheat oven to 250°F. In a large casserole or deep skillet with ovenproof lid, over medium-high heat, heat oil. Add chicken pieces, season with salt and pepper and cook until underside is golden, 5–7 minutes. Turn chicken pieces and add remaining ingredients, stirring well.

3 Cover pan tightly and bake, basting occasionally, for 1½–2 hours, adding a little more chicken stock or water if all liquid has been absorbed.

4 To serve, arrange the chicken pieces on a serving platter and pour any juices over; garnish with parsley sprigs.

Creole Chicken

Serves 4

- 2 tbsp. chopped onion
- 4 tsp. fresh thyme or 1 tsp. dried
- 2 tsp. salt
- 2 tsp. ground nutmeg
- 4 tsp. sugar
- 2 tsp. fresh ground black pepper
- 6 oz. half chicken breasts, boned, skinned and fat cut off
- 1 tbsp. butter or margarine
- 1 tbsp. oil

This dish leans toward sweet and spicy and is not hot at all. Serve with pigeon peas and rice.

1 Combine the onion, thyme, salt, nutmeg, sugar, and black pepper in a small bowl or in a food processor.

2 Prick the chicken breasts several times with a knife point, place in a non-reactive bowl and rub the mixture over both sides of each breast. Cover and refrigerate for about 20 minutes.

3 Heat the butter or margarine and oil in a skillet that will accommodate the breasts in a single layer. Add the chicken and fry gently on each side for 5–10 minutes, depending on thickness. The chicken is done when the juices run clear.

Bajan Breaded Fried Chicken

Serves 4

- 4 chicken breasts
- 3 tbsp. stemmed, seeded and finely chopped chiles
- 6 scallions, finely chopped (including tops)
- 3 cloves garlic, minced
- 2 tbsp. lime juice
- 2 tbsp. chopped fresh cilantro
- 1 tbsp. chopped fresh chives
- ½ tsp. ground cloves
- ¼ tsp. thyme
- ¼ tsp. marjoram
- ¼ tsp paprika
- ½ tsp. freshly ground black pepper
- 1 egg
- 1 tbsp. soy sauce
- 1 tbsp. hot pepper sauce
- flour for dredging
- 3 cups dry bread crumbs
- vegetable oil for frying

Bajans rub jerk seasoning into slits cut in the chicken and then the chicken is breaded and fried.

1 Bake or microwave the chicken breasts until tender. If microwaving, cover with wax paper and microwave on full for 13–15 minutes or until the breasts are no longer pink, rearranging them at 5 minute intervals. If pre-baking, preheat the oven to 350°F, brush the chicken with vegetable oil or clarified butter, place in a shallow baking pan and bake until tender, about 30 minutes. Set aside to cool.

2 Combine the chiles, scallions, garlic, lime juice, cilantro, chives, cloves, thyme, marjoram, paprika, and black pepper. Cut deep gashes in the chicken and fill with the mixture.

3 Beat together the egg, soy sauce, and hot pepper sauce. Lightly dust the chicken with the flour, dip in the egg mixture and roll in the bread crumbs.

4 Heat the oil to 375°F and fry the chicken until golden brown, about 4 minutes on each side. Drain on paper towels and serve.

Stuffed Chicken Wings

Serves 4

- 8 chicken wings

Stuffing

- ¼ lb. bean thread vermicelli
- 3 pieces dark wood ear fungus
- 1¼ cups ground pork
- 1 small onion, finely grated
- 1 small carrot, finely grated
- 1 egg, beaten
- 1 tbsp. light soy sauce
- salt and black pepper

This is a delicious and economical dish from Vietnam which looks very impressive.

1 Bone the chicken wings by cutting around the bone with a sharp knife. Holding the wingtip, gently ease the bone away to leave the skin and a thin layer of chicken.

2 Soak the vermicelli in warm water for 10 minutes then drain thoroughly and cut into short strands. Soak the wood ear fungus in warm water for 10 minutes then squeeze dry and chop into thin slices.

3 Mix the stuffing ingredients together. The mixture should be firm. Mold the stuffing into a ball and insert it into the bag of flesh and skin of the chicken wings.

4 Preheat the oven to 400°F. Steam the stuffed wings for 10–15 minutes. (If you want to make a large quantity, multiply the measures accordingly and freeze after the steaming stage.)

5 After steaming, place in a lightly oiled roasting pan and roast in the oven for 30 minutes. Serve on a bed of lettuce as a starter or with rice and a stir-fried dish.

Citrus-Fried Chicken

Serves 4

- 1 chicken, cut up
- ¼ cup fresh lime juice
- ¼ cup fresh lemon juice
- ¼ cup fresh orange juice
- ¼ cup olive oil
- 4 cloves garlic, minced
- few drops of hot pepper sauce
- 1 cup flour
- 1 tsp. salt
- ½ tsp. black pepper
- vegetable oil or shortening

From Florida, with its Caribbean influences, comes the inspiration for this tangy, crispy fried chicken. It is marinated in a mix of lemon, lime, and orange juices, spiced with garlic and hot pepper sauce. For the best flavor, use freshly squeezed juices.

1 Make the marinade by mixing fruit juices, olive oil, garlic and hot pepper sauce. Trim any excess fat off the chicken and remove skin, if desired. Put the chicken pieces in a glass or other non-reactive dish. Pour the marinade over the chicken, making sure that each piece is coated. Marinate in refrigerator at least 3 hours, or overnight.

2 Mix flour, salt and pepper in a bowl or a paper bag. Dip each chicken piece in the mixture to give it a thin coating of flour.

3 Heat oil or lard in a heavy skillet. The oil should be about ½–1 inch deep, and very hot. Carefully place chicken in the hot oil. The pieces should not be crowded. You probably will need to fry the chicken in two batches (keep the first batch warm in the oven while the second is cooking), or use two skillets. Fry over medium or medium-high heat, depending on your stove and the heaviness of the skillet. Watch carefully so that the chicken does not burn. It is done when the meat juices run clear, about 20–25 minutes.

Cochin-style Chili Chicken

Serves 4

- 2 tbsp. lemon juice
- 1 tsp. salt
- 2 tbsp. sugar
- 2 tbsp. vegetable oil
- 10–12 fresh or dried curry leaves or 1 tsp. curry powder
- ¼ lb. shallots, sliced
- 6 cloves garlic, finely chopped
- 1 inch piece fresh ginger root, finely chopped
- 5 medium-hot green chiles, seeded and very finely sliced
- 2 medium tomatoes, chopped
- ½ tsp. turmeric
- ¼ tsp. chili powder
- 3–3½ lb. chicken, jointed into 8
- 2 tbsp. chopped fresh cilantro

Garnish
- fresh cilantro leaves
- lemon wedges

This recipe is based on a dish which comes from the Jewish community in Cochin, in southern India. Hot boiled rice is the ideal accompaniment.

1 In a small bowl, place lemon juice, ¼ tsp. salt and sugar; stir to dissolve. Set aside.

2 In a casserole or large deep skillet, over medium-high heat, heat oil. Add curry leaves or curry powder and stir until they sizzle, 10–15 seconds. Stir in shallots, garlic, ginger, and chiles and cook until the shallots have softened and begin to color, 5–7 minutes. Stir in tomatoes, turmeric, chili powder, and remaining salt. Cook 3–4 minutes longer.

3 Add chicken to the vegetable mixture, moving pieces around to cover with some vegetables. Stir in 1 cup water and bring just to a boil. Reduce heat to low and cook, covered tightly, 20 minutes, stirring once.

4 Uncover and stir in reserved lemon-juice mixture and chopped cilantro. Increase heat to medium and cook, uncovered, until sauce is slightly reduced, basting chicken occasionally with the sauce (about 10 minutes).

5 Arrange chicken pieces on a serving platter. Pour sauce over and garnish with cilantro leaves and lemon wedges.

Mustard Baked Chicken

Serves 6-8

- ½ cup sour cream
- ¼ cup Creole mustard
- 6 oz. finely crumbled cornbread
- 1½ tsp. fresh thyme or ½ tsp. dried thyme
- 1 tsp. salt
- ¼ tsp. black pepper
- ¼ tsp. cayenne
- 2 chickens, about 2½–3 lb. each, cut into serving pieces
- 5 tbsp. butter

Coated with cornbread crumbs and a sauce of mustard and sour cream, this chicken dish is easy and tasty.

1 In a small bowl, combine the sour cream and mustard. In another bowl, mix together the cornbread crumbs and seasonings.

2 Spread the mustard mixture over the chicken pieces, then roll the chicken in the crumb mixture. Arrange the chicken in a single layer in a large, shallow baking dish and drizzle with the melted butter. Bake at 375°F until the chicken is golden brown and the juices run clear if tested with the tip of a knife, about 1 hour.

Spanish Chicken with Tomatoes, Pepper and Cumin

Serves 2

- 🪶 *1 Rock Cornish game hen, about 1½ lb., or 2 chicken legs*
- 🪶 *salt and freshly ground black pepper*
- 🪶 *2 tbsp. olive oil*
- 🪶 *2 onions, chopped*
- 🪶 *4 large tomatoes, chopped*
- 🪶 *1 green pepper, seeded and chopped*
- 🪶 *2 bayleaves*
- 🪶 *1 tsp. cumin seeds*
- 🪶 *2 cloves garlic, finely chopped*

A simple, spicy summer lunch for two, this recipe originally comes from Spain.

1 Split the bird, cutting the backbone free, and rub salt and pepper into the flesh. Heat the oil in a small casserole and color the chicken on the skin side while you prepare the vegetables.

2 Add the onions, tomatoes, and pepper as they are prepared, tucking in the backbone (if using a game hen) and bayleaf. Cover and cook over a low heat for 15–20 minutes.

3 Meanwhile, grind the cumin seeds in a mortar, working in the chopped garlic. Remove the backbone, stir the vegetables gently and work in the cumin paste.

4 Cook for another 3–4 minutes, to allow the flavors to blend. Serve with the chicken skin upwards.

Sweet, Sour 'n' Hot Chicken

Serves 4

- ½ cup marmalade
- ½ cup lime juice
- 1 tsp. chopped fresh root ginger
- 1 tsp. ground nutmeg
- dash hot pepper sauce
- 1 tbsp. vegetable oil
- 4 large chicken breasts (about 1½ lb.) boned, skinned, fat cut off, cut into 1 inch cubes
- 1 medium papaya (pawpaw), seeded, halved and cut into 1 inch cubes
- 1½ cups can sliced water chestnuts, drained

Garnish

- ½ oz. fresh cilantro, chopped

1 In a small saucepan, melt the marmalade over a low heat, gradually blending in the lime juice, ginger, nutmeg, and hot pepper sauce.

2 Heat the oil in a skillet and brown the chicken cubes. Add the papaya and toss for several minutes, then add the sauce and water chestnuts. Cook over a moderate heat for about 3–4 minutes until the chicken is cooked through. Taste the sauce and add hot pepper sauce to taste.

5 Spoon on to a serving dish and sprinkle with cilantro.

Chiles with Chicken

Serves 4

- 1 lb. cooked chicken or turkey
- 4 poblano chiles
- 1 large red onion, chopped
- 2–3 tbsp. shortening or olive oil
- 1 cup sour cream
- 1½–2 cups grated Cheddar or Jack cheese
- salt and pepper

1 You can use any leftover cooked poultry, diced or shredded; the super-deluxe version of this dish uses shredded chicken breasts.

2 Blister and peel the chiles. Remove veins and seeds; dice.

3 Cook the onion in the oil or shortening until it is translucent. Add the chicken and the chiles. Cook until both are warm, stirring frequently (about 5 minutes).

4 Add the sour cream and grated cheese. Season to taste. Stir constantly until the cheese melts (about 2–3 minutes).

Turmeric Chicken

Serves 6

- 4 tbsp. vegetable oil
- 6 chicken leg portions, approx. 7 oz. each
- 2 medium onions, chopped
- 1 tbsp. ground coriander
- 1 tsp. turmeric
- 1 tsp. ground cumin
- ½ tsp. ground cardamom
- 2 dashes hot chili powder
- 2 tbsp. all-purpose flour
- 3 cups chicken stock
- ½ cup blanched almonds, coarsely chopped
- ½ cup dates, pitted and coarsely chopped
- ⅔ cup natural low fat yogurt or fromage frais
- 2 tbsp. chopped fresh cilantro
- salt

Very spicy, and full of Eastern promise – cardamom, dates, almonds and the characteristic yellow turmeric – this is best accompanied with plain boiled rice and a refreshing cucumber or tomato salad to calm down the palate!

1 Heat the oil in a pan, and sauté the chicken legs until golden brown. Remove to one side.

2 Add the onion to the pan and sauté until golden brown. Reduce the heat and stir in the spices. Cook for 1 minute.

3 Add the chicken legs. Sprinkle in the flour and blend in the stock. Bring to a boil, then simmer for 30 minutes, or until the chicken is tender.

4 Mix in the almonds, dates, yogurt, and half the fresh cilantro. Simmer gently for a further 10 minutes.

5 Serve hot, garnished with the remaining cilantro.

Malaysian Chicken Curry

Serves 4

- 2 tbsp. ground coriander
- 1 tbsp. ground cumin
- 2 tsp. turmeric
- 1 tsp. ground cinnamon
- 1 tsp. chili powder
- ½ tsp. grated nutmeg
- 8 small chicken joints (wings, thighs, drumsticks), skinned
- 4 tbsp. vegetable oil
- ½ lb. onions, finely chopped
- 1 oz. fresh ginger, peeled and chopped
- 2 cloves garlic, chopped
- 2 cardamom pods (seeds only)
- 4 cloves
- 1 tsp. dried chiles
- 2½ cups hot chicken stock
- 1 lb. potatoes, peeled and cut into chunks
- 1 lb. carrots, peeled and cut into chunks
- 1 cup hot milk
- 1⅓ cups shredded coconut
- 2 tbsp. cornstarch
- 1 tbsp. lemon juice
- 1 tbsp. black treacle

Garnish

- chopped fresh cilantro

This curry is a complete meal on its own – it includes carrots and potatoes, but cauliflower and string or snap beans would also be good. Accompany with poppadums and a fresh tomato salad to cool the palate!

1 Mix the first six ingredients together in a bowl, and add the dry chicken joints. Mix well, rubbing the spices into the surface of the chicken.

2 Heat the oil in a large heavy-based pan, and fry the onions, ginger, and garlic until softened and golden. Add the cardamom seeds, cloves, chiles, and any loose powder from the chicken spice mix. Cook for a further minute, scraping the bottom of the pan well.

3 Add the chicken and cook, turning occasionally, for 3–4 minutes or until the surface of the chicken seals. Pour over the hot stock and a little salt, to taste. Cover and simmer for 15–20 minutes.

4 Stir in the potato and carrot chunks, cover and simmer for a further 40 minutes.

5 Meanwhile, pour the hot milk over the shredded coconut and leave to infuse for ½ hour. Squeeze the liquid through a fine sieve or cheesecloth. Blend with the cornstarch and lemon juice and stir into the curry. Simmer, uncovered, until thickened.

6 Stir in the treacle. Correct seasoning and serve, garnished with freshly chopped cilantro.

Chicken Kashmir

Serves 4

- 1½ lb. boneless chicken, cubed (breast or thigh)
- ⅔ cup natural yogurt
- 1 tsp. ground coriander
- 1 tsp. ground cumin
- 1 tsp. ground cinnamon
- ½ tsp. coriander seeds
- ½ tsp. ground ginger
- salt
- 1 tbsp. vegetable oil
- 1 medium onion, sliced
- 1 clove garlic, finely chopped
- 1 tbsp. all-purpose flour
- 6 tbsp. chicken stock
- 1 oz. creamed coconut
- 3 tbsp. chopped fresh cilantro

Garnish

- ¼ cup flaked almonds, toasted

For those who like a milder, more subtle Indian dish, this is ideal. The selected spices are warm rather than hot and the sauce is creamy.

1 Cut the chicken into bite-size pieces. Place in a bowl with the yogurt, coriander, cumin, cinnamon, coriander seeds, ground ginger, and a little salt and stir until well coated. Cover and chill for 4 hours, but preferably overnight.

2 Heat the oil in a pan, add the onion and garlic and sauté until softened and golden. Strain the chicken pieces and add to the pan. Sauté until sealed.

3 Sprinkle on the flour, then blend in the chicken stock. Add the creamed coconut and stir until it dissolves and the mixture thickens.

4 Pour in the remaining yogurt and spice marinade. Cover and simmer for 25 minutes or until the chicken is tender. Adjust seasoning, if necessary.

5 Five minutes before the end, stir in the chopped cilantro.

6 Serve the chicken sprinkled with the toasted almonds and accompanied with rice.

Creamy Coconut Chicken Curry

Serves 4

- ⅔ cup boiling water
- ⅔ cup milk
- 1⅓ cups shredded coconut
- 2 tbsp. groundnut oil
- 3 lb. chicken, jointed and skinned
- 2 onions, finely chopped
- 1 clove garlic, finely chopped
- 2 tsp. grated fresh ginger
- 2 tbsp. mild curry powder
- 2 tbsp. all-purpose flour
- 1¼ cups chicken stock
- ⅓ cup golden raisins
- ⅔ cup flaked coconut
- 1 tsp. salt
- 1 tbsp. lemon juice
- 6 tbsp. natural yogurt

The subtle coconut flavor is obtained by infusing shredded coconut in milk or water. This needs to be prepared in advance, but will result in an authentic addition to curries. Serve this creamy curry with plain boiled rice and a banana or tomato salad.

1 Pour in the boiling water and milk over the shredded coconut in a bowl. Stir and leave to infuse for about 2 hours. Strain the liquid, squeezing well, and discard the coconut.

2 Heat the oil in a pan, add the chicken pieces a few at a time, and cook until golden brown, for 6–8 minutes. Remove to one side.

3 Add the onions and garlic and ginger to the pan and cook for 1 minute. Sprinkle on the curry powder and flour and cook, stirring to a paste, for a further minute.

4 Gradually blend in the stock and coconut milk and slowly bring to a boil, stirring, until thickened.

5 Return the chicken to the pan together with the golden raisins and flaked coconut. Cover and simmer for 25 minutes.

6 Remove lid and simmer for a further 15 minutes or until the sauce has reduced and thickened slightly more. Add the lemon juice and salt, to taste.

7 Remove the pan from the heat, swirl in the yogurt and serve immediately.

Curried Chicken with Mangoes

Serves 4

- 2 tbsp. vegetable oil
- ½ lb. onions, sliced
- 2 tbsp. hot curry powder
- ¼ cup all-purpose flour
- 1 large can mangoes in light syrup, approximately 13 oz.
- chicken stock
- ⅔ cup raisins
- 1 tbsp. shredded coconut
- ½ tsp. salt
- 1 lb. cooked chicken, cut into bite-size pieces

This is a quick, convenient way of using up cooked chicken meat by making it stretch into another delicious meal. Canned mangoes are used as a convenience, but can be substituted with what suits your store cupboard – pineapple and peaches are just as good.

1 Heat the oil in a large saucepan. Add the onions and sauté until softened and just turning golden.

2 Stir in the curry powder and flour and cook for a further minute.

3 Drain the mangoes. Measure the juice and make up to 3 cups with the chicken stock. Cut the fruit into bite-size pieces.

4 Blend the stock into the onion mixture, and bring to a boil, stirring. Add the raisins, coconut and salt.

5 Stir in the chicken meat, cover and simmer for 30 minutes. Five minutes before the end, add the pieces of mango.

6 Serve accompanied with plain boiled rice and poppadums.
Note: Do not reheat this dish.

Red Chicken Curry

Serves 6

- 5 cups thin coconut milk
- 10 white peppercorns, crushed
- ¾ lb. boneless skinned chicken breasts, cut across into ¼ inch thick slices
- 3 tbsp. fish sauce
- ½ tbsp. palm sugar
- 7 small white eggplants, quartered
- 3 fresh red chiles, quartered lengthwise
- 2 kaffir lime leaves, torn into small pieces
- ¾ oz. sweet basil leaves

Chili Paste
- 5 dried red chiles, chopped roughly
- 1½ tsp. sliced shallots
- ½ tbsp. finely sliced lemon grass
- ½ tbsp. chopped garlic
- 2 tsp. salt
- 1 tsp. shrimp paste
- 1 tsp. sliced fresh ginger

- ½ tsp. chopped lime or lemon zest
- ½ tsp. chopped cilantro root or stem

In Thailand this curry is served in bowls accompanied by rice, sun-dried beef, and salted preserved eggs.

1 Heat 1 cup of the coconut milk in a pan, stir in the chili paste and white peppercorns, and cook for 2 minutes.

2 Add the chicken slices, mix well and add the rest of the coconut milk. Bring to a boil, then add the fish sauce and palm sugar.

3 Boil for 1 minute and then add the eggplant, chili, and lime leaf. Bring back a boil, cook for 3 minutes, add the basil, remove from the heat and serve.

Tangy Lime Juice and Garlic Chicken Wings

Serves 6

- 🌺 *12 chicken wings*
- 🌺 *4 cloves garlic, minced*
- 🌺 *salt and freshly ground black pepper, to taste*
- 🌺 *freshly squeezed juice of 4 limes*
- 🌺 *dash cayenne pepper*

Whenever you buy a whole chicken, freeze the wings if they are not needed. When you have enough in the freezer you can transform them into this deliciously tangy recipe.

1 Place the chicken wings in a shallow dish. Rub the minced garlic all over the chicken wings, then season with salt and freshly ground black pepper.

2 Sprinkle the lime juice and cayenne pepper over the chicken wings, cover, and marinate in the refrigerator for 3–4 hours, turning and rearranging them occasionally.

3 Arrange the chicken wings in a large skillet and pour the marinade over them. Add just enough cold water to cover the wings and bring quickly to a boil. Cook, uncovered, for 20–25 minutes, or until the chicken is cooked through and the sauce has reduced slightly. Serve warm or, better still, cold the next day.

Tahini Garlic Chicken Wings

Serves 6

- 12–18 chicken wings, tips trimmed off
- 2 tsp. paprika
- 1 tsp. ground cumin
- 3–4 cloves garlic, minced
- salt and freshly ground pepper
- juice of 1 lemon
- 4–5 tbsp. olive oil

Tahini Garlic Sauce
- 2 cloves garlic, minced
- ¼ tsp. salt
- large dash cayenne
- 1 cup tahini paste
- ⅔ cup lemon juice

Tahini is the most frequently encountered Lebanese sauce. It is served hot or cold with fish and vegetables. It bears a resemblance to Indonesian peanut sauce (*gado-gado*) in its nuttiness.

1 Wash the chicken wings and pat dry. Rub in the paprika and cumin with your hands. In a small bowl, mash the garlic cloves with salt and pepper to taste, then whisk in the lemon juice and oil until combined. Pour over the chicken wings in a shallow dish, turning to coat them.

2 Cook the wings under a medium-hot preheated broiler, turning occasionally, until done. Turn and baste the wings with the marinade until they are tender, but cooked inside and golden brown and slightly charred outside.

3 To make the Tahini Garlic Sauce, mash the garlic in a bowl with the salt and cayenne until it makes a paste. Whisk in the tahini paste with a fork, then thin the mixture with the juice beating continuously. Serve the sauce immediately or cover and chill. (The sauce can be kept refrigerated for 2 weeks, and it can also be frozen.) Spoon Tahini Garlic Sauce over each wing and serve piping hot.

Spiced Bean Chicken

Serves 4

- 1 cup mixed dried pulses (red kidney beans, garbanzo peas, navy beans etc)
- 1 clove garlic, finely chopped
- 1 medium onion, finely chopped
- 2 tbsp. vegetable oil
- ½ tsp. turmeric
- ½ tsp. ground cumin
- 8 medium chicken drumsticks
- salt and freshly ground black pepper
- 6 tomatoes, seeded and chopped
- 2½ cups chicken stock
- ¼ lb. okra

Garnish

- freshly chopped parsley

A feast full of protein with an Eastern flavor, serve with some naan bread and a crisp fresh salad.

1 Soak the pulses in cold water overnight. Drain and put into a pan with enough fresh cold water to cover well, and boil steadily for 10 minutes. Drain thoroughly.

2 Heat the oil in a large saucepan, add the onion and garlic and cook gently until softened.

3 Add the spices and cook for a further minute then add the chicken drumsticks. Season to taste. Cook, stirring for 5 minutes until the chicken is coated with the spices.

4 Add the tomatoes, stock, and drained pulses, cover and simmer gently for 45–60 minutes or until the beans are tender.

5 Add the okra 5 minutes before the end of cooking.

6 Serve piping hot sprinkled with fresh chopped parsley.

Cubano Chicken

Serves 4-6

- 6 large whole chicken legs with thighs, or 4 large half chicken breasts with wings attached or detached
- 2 cloves garlic, finely chopped
- ¼ tsp. salt
- ¼ tsp. freshly ground black pepper
- ½ tsp. marjoram
- ½ tsp. ground cumin
- ½ cup Seville orange juice or ¼ cup orange juice and ¼ cup lime juice
- 1 large onion, thinly sliced
- ¼ cup vegetable oil

Cuban food is not hot but it is well seasoned and flavorful. If you would like to make this dish a little hotter – the way it is enjoyed in the Dominican Republic and Puerto Rico – chop up a small chili and add it when you toss the reserved marinade into the pot.

1 Arrange the chicken in a single layer in a large baking dish.

2 Combine the garlic, salt, pepper, marjoram, cumin, pepper, and orange juice. Mix well and spoon evenly over the chicken.

3 Top with onion slices, cover and marinate for at least 2 hours or overnight in the refrigerator, turning the chicken occasionally.

4 Remove the baking dish from the refrigerator 1 hour before cooking. Drain the chicken, reserving the marinade and pat dry with paper towels.

5 In a large skillet, heat the vegetable oil over medium heat. Add the chicken and fry until brown, about 5 minutes per side. Add the marinade and onions. Reduce the heat to low and cook for 25 minutes.

Sautéed Chicken Compote

Serves 4

- 4 large half chicken breasts, boned, skinned and cut in ½ inch strips
- about ½ cup curry powder
- ¼ cup clarified butter
- 1 ripe papaya peeled, seeded (seeds reserved) and cut into ¼ inch chunks
- 2 bananas, sliced crosswise ¼ inch thick
- ⅓ cup unsweetened coconut flakes, toasted
- ½ cup dark rum
- ⅓ cup coconut cream
- ½ tsp. salt
- ½ tsp. white pepper

1 Dredge the chicken strips in curry powder.

2 Melt the clarified butter in a large skillet over high heat. Stir in the chicken and sauté until golden brown. Add the papaya, bananas, and coconut flakes. Add the rum, which will ignite, and let the alcohol burn off.

3 Add the cream of coconut and simmer until heated then season with salt and pepper. Stir quickly.

4 Serve immediately with a chilled green salad topped with your favorite vinaigrette and sprinkled with papaya seeds.

Rum Marinated Chicken

Serves 4

- 3 tbsp. dark rum
- 3 tbsp. soy sauce
- 3 tbsp. lime juice
- 4 lb. chicken, cut into 16 pieces
- 1 clove garlic, minced
- ½ tsp. salt
- freshly ground black pepper
- 2 cups all-purpose flour
- vegetable oil for deep frying

1 Warm the rum in a small pan over a low heat. Remove the pan from the heat, and set light to the rum with a match. Shake the pan back and forth until the flame dies. Add the soy sauce and lime juice to the rum.

2 Put the chicken pieces in a bowl, and pour the rum mixture over them. Add the garlic, mix it in well, then let marinate for 4 hours, turning the pieces now and then.

3 Preheat the oven to its lowest temperature, and line a heatproof dish with aluminum foil.

4 Heat some oil in a big skillet. Pat the chicken pieces dry with paper towels, and then season with the salt and freshly ground black pepper. Dip the pieces in the flour, shaking them to remove any excess, and then fry them. When the pieces are golden brown, transfer them to the prepared dish and keep them warm in the oven.

5 Serve with hot boiled rice and a mixed vegetable stew.

Buttermilk Chicken

Serves 4

- 3–3½ lb. chicken, cut into portions
- 3 cups buttermilk
- ½ cup dry bread crumbs
- ¼ cup cornmeal
- scant ½ cup grated Parmesan cheese
- ½ tsp. dried marjoram
- 1 tsp. paprika
- ¼ tsp. garlic powder
- ½ tsp. salt
- ¼ tsp. pepper

This chicken is marinated in buttermilk, which gives it a subtle tang reminiscent of sour cream. It is then coated in a tasty mixture of crumbs, Parmesan cheese and spices, and baked. It's an easy and delicious alternative to fried chicken.

1 Trim fat and any excess skin off chicken pieces. Put the pieces in a glass, ceramic or plastic bowl, and pour the buttermilk over them. Let the chicken soak in the buttermilk all day or overnight.

2 Preheat oven to 400°F. Lightly grease a 9 x 13 inch baking pan or dish.

3 Mix the remaining ingredients. Remove chicken from the buttermilk and let it drain briefly. Dip each piece in the crumb mixture and pat crumbs on any bare spots.

4 Place the chicken in a baking dish, making sure not to crowd the pieces. Bake until the chicken is golden brown and the juices run clear instead of pink, for 40–50 minutes.

Russian Chicken Cutlets

Serves 6

- *1½ lb chicken, finely chopped, well chilled*
- *2 cups fresh bread crumbs*
- *6 tbsp. unsalted butter, softened*
- *½ cup heavy cream*
- *large dash nutmeg*
- *salt and freshly ground black pepper*
- *2 large eggs, beaten*
- *2 tbsp. vegetable oil*

Mustard Sauce

- *4 tbsp. unsalted butter*
- *1 small onion, chopped*
- *1 cup dry white wine*
- *1 cup chicken stock*
- *2 tsp. flour*
- *2 tbsp. Dijon-style mustard*
- *2 tbsp. fresh lemon juice or sour cream*

These patties are encountered all over Russia and are frequently served with the mustard sauce given here.

1. In a blender or a food processor, combine the chopped chicken with ¾ cup breadcrumbs, ¼ cup butter, the cream, nutmeg, and salt and pepper to taste. Process until the mixture reaches the consistency of paste. Remove, form into 6 cutlet-shaped patties, and place on wax paper. Chill for at least 2 hours.

2. Meanwhile, start the sauce. In a stainless steel or enamel saucepan, melt 4 tsp. butter, and gently sauté the onion until it is softened. Stir in the white wine and the stock,and bring to a boil. Reduce the heat and simmer,uncovered, for about 10 minutes, then set aside.

3. Using your fingers, knead the flour into the remaining butter. Increase the heat of the stock and drop in the flour and butter mixture bit by bit, stirring all the time. When the sauce is thickened, remove from the heat.

4. Take the cutlets from the refrigerator. Place the beaten eggs in a shallow bowl and the remaining bread crumbs on a plate. Dip each of the cutlets into the beaten egg, shaking off the excess, and then press into the bread crumbs, coating each side well. Chill for another hour.

5. Heat the remaining butter and the oil in a large saucepan and fry the cutlets, 3 at a time, over medium-high heat for 4–5 minutes each side, or until golden brown and cooked through. Remove and keep warm.

6. Finish the sauce by reheating it gently, stirring. Stir in the mustard and lemon juice or sour cream.

Greek-style Chicken

Serves 4

- *4 chicken leg portions*
- *2 medium red-skinned onions, peeled and quartered*
- *4 cloves garlic, chopped*
- *2 lemons, cut into chunks*
- *¾ lb. new potatoes, scrubbed and halved*
- *1 tbsp. chopped fresh thyme or 1 tsp. dried thyme*
- *4 tbsp. olive oil*
- *salt and freshly ground black pepper*

Garnish

- *freshly chopped thyme (optional)*

Serve this fragrant dish piping hot with a crisp salad and a bowl of yogurt dressing, such as tzatsiki.

1. Cut the chicken leg portions in half with a meat cleaver or very sharp knife. (Follow the fine white line on the underside of the leg.)

2. Place the chicken into a large shallow ovenproof dish with the onions, garlic, lemon, potatoes, thyme, half the olive oil, and a little salt and pepper.

3. Drizzle over the remaining olive oil, cover with foil, and cook for 30 minutes at 375°F, stirring once or twice, until the chicken is tender and the potatoes and onions are a good color.

4. Serve hot, garnished, if you like, with a sprinkling of freshly chopped thyme.

Sesame Garbanzo Beans with Chicken

Serves 4

- 1 lettuce heart, shredded
- 2 inch piece cucumber, peeled and diced
- 1 bunch of radishes, sliced
- 3 tbsp. roasted sesame seeds
- 6 tbsp. olive oil
- 15 oz. cans garbanzo beans, drained
- 1 lb. cooked chicken, diced
- ½ cup tahini
- 6 tbsp. snipped chives
- 3 tbsp. chopped fresh parsley
- salt and freshly ground black pepper

- 2 avocados, halved, pitted, peeled and cut in chunks
- 1 cup pitted black olives, halved

Garnish

- 1 lemon, cut into wedges

Transform leftover cooked chicken into a tasty meal. In fact this recipe may be used for any cooked meat.

1 Mix the lettuce, cucumber, radishes, and sesame seeds, then arrange this salad around the edge of four serving plates or one large dish.

2 Heat the oil, then stir-fry the garbanzo beans and chicken for about 5 minutes, or until the chicken is thoroughly heated. Stir in the tahini until it combines with the oil to coat the ingredients in a creamy dressing. Add the herbs, seasoning, and avocados, then stir the black olives into the mixture.

3 Divide the chicken mixture between the serving plates and garnish with lemon wedges. The lemon juice should be squeezed over the chicken mixture and salad.

Lemon Marmalade Chicken

Serves 4

- 4 boneless half chicken breasts, skinned
- 3 tbsp. all-purpose flour
- salt and freshly ground black pepper
- 1 tbsp. sunflower oil
- 4 tbsp. butter
- 1 bayleaf
- 1 thyme sprig
- grated zest and juice of 1 large lemon
- 6 tbsp. lemon marmalade

Garnish

- lemon slices, thyme sprigs (optional)

This zesty chicken dish is extremely simple and it tastes terrific with new potatoes and a crisp salad.

1 Slice the chicken breasts across into large medallions, then toss the pieces in the flour and plenty of seasoning.

2 Heat the oil and half the butter, then stir-fry the bayleaf, thyme, and chicken until golden and cooked through. Add the lemon zest and juice and continue cooking for about 30 seconds, while stirring, to coat the chicken with lemon.

3 Next add the marmalade with 3 tbsp. water and stir until the marmalade has dissolved, and has combined with the other ingredients to form a bubbling glaze. Stir in the remaining butter to give the glaze a good gloss and to enrich the dish. Serve at once, garnished with lemon slices and thyme, if wished.

Creole-style Roast Chicken

Serves 6

- ½ cup butter or margarine
- 1 small clove garlic, peeled
- 1½ cups soft, fresh bread crumbs
- 3 tbsp. lime juice
- 2 tsp. finely grated lime rind
- 4 tbsp. dark rum
- 1 tsp. brown sugar
- ¼ tsp. ground cinnamon
- ¼ tsp. cayenne pepper
- 1 tsp. salt
- freshly ground black pepper
- 3 ripe bananas
- 4 lb. chicken, turkey or goose
- 1¼ cups chicken stock

The recipe for this spicy stuffing has its origins in Haiti.

1 Preheat oven to 350°F.

2 Melt half the butter or margarine in a small skillet, then add the garlic and stir it around the pan for 10 seconds. Remove and discard the garlic. Add the bread crumbs, two-thirds of the lime juice, the lime rind, a quarter of the rum, the sugar, cinnamon, cayenne pepper, salt and freshly ground black pepper to taste. Mix well, and set the stuffing on one side.

3 Peel and chop the bananas, then put them in a bowl. Add the remaining lime juice, 2 tbsp. rum, and salt and freshly ground black pepper to taste. Mix well together. Stuff the chicken or other fowl with the banana stuffing, and sew the opening closed with a large needle and trussing string.

4 Fill the small neck cavity with the bread crumb stuffing and sew up the opening in the same way as before.

5 Brush the chicken with the remaining butter or margarine. Place it in a roasting pan, and roast in the preheated oven for 1 hour, basting occasionally with the juices.

6 After removing the chicken from the oven, transfer it to a large heated dish and leave it to rest for 5 minutes, as this makes it easier to carve. Meanwhile, skim the fat from the juices left in the roasting pan, and pour in the chicken stock. Bring to a boil over a high heat, stirring all the time. Cook for 2 minutes, taste for seasoning, and pour into a sauceboat.

7 Just before serving, warm the last tablespoons of rum in a small pan. Remove it from the heat, then set light to the rum with a match and pour it, flaming, over the chicken. Serve immediately.

McJerk Nuggets

Serves 4

- 2 lb. chicken thighs and/or breasts, skinned and chopped into 2 inch cubes

Jerk Seasoning

- 2 tsp. chili powder
- 1½ tsp. ground cumin
- ½ tsp. cayenne pepper
- 2 tsp. salt

Serve this with a rice or pasta dish for a meal the children especially will love. The cubes can be cut in quarters when cold and served in a Caesar salad instead of anchovies.

1 Rinse and drain the chicken cubes and pat dry with paper towels. Place in a bowl and rub in the Jerk Seasoning. Place in a heavy-duty, sealable, plastic food storage bag or a non-reactive bowl, covered, and let marinate for at least 1 hour or overnight in the refrigerator.

2 Preheat the oven to 350°F. Place the chicken pieces in a roasting pan and bake, covered, until chicken is done (about 45 minutes), turning the chicken halfway through the cooking time.

3 Just before removing the chicken from the oven, mix 1–2 tsp. of Jerk Seasoning with some of the juices in the pan and a small amount of water to thin the sauce if necessary. Spoon over the cooked chicken and serve.

Walnut and Pear Stuffed Roast Chicken

Serves 6

- 🥄 1 small ripe pear, peeled, cored and chopped
- 🥄 1 cup fresh wholewheat bread crumbs
- 🥄 ¼ cup chopped walnuts
- 🥄 generous dash ground ginger
- 🥄 salt and freshly ground black pepper
- 🥄 1 egg yolk
- 🥄 5 cloves
- 🥄 ½ lemon
- 🥄 3½ lb. chicken
- 🥄 2 tbsp. clear honey

Garnish

- 🥄 1 pear, cored and sliced
- 🥄 1 tbsp. clear honey

Pears are often neglected in savory cooking, but here they prove their worth in a delicious nutty stuffing.

1 Mix the chopped pear with the bread crumbs, walnuts, ginger, and salt and pepper to taste. Mix in the egg yolk to bind the stuffing together.

2 Push the cloves into the skin of the half lemon and place inside the chicken.

3 Press the pear stuffing into the neck cavity of the chicken and fold the remaining neck skin neatly underneath the bird, to secure the stuffing.

4 Place the chicken in a roasting dish, season with salt and pepper, and brush all over with honey. Cook in a preheated oven at 400°F for 1¼–1½ hours. Baste several times during cooking, spooning the honeyed juices over the chicken.

5 To prepare the glazed pears for the garnish, gently heat together the pear slices and the honey in the pan, turning the pears from time to time until they become translucent.

6 To serve, carve or joint the bird and serve accompanied with some stuffing and a few glazed pear slices.

Spiced Spatchcock

Serves 2

- 🥄 2 Rock Cornish game hens, approx. 1 lb. each
- 🥄 grated rind and juice 1 small lemon
- 🥄 1 tbsp. olive oil
- 🥄 1 shallot or small sweet onion, finely chopped
- 🥄 1 clove garlic, finely chopped
- 🥄 2 tsp. green peppercorns, crushed
- 🥄 1 tsp. coriander seeds, crushed
- 🥄 4 juniper berries, crushed
- 🥄 ½ tsp. ground allspice
- 🥄 2 sprigs rosemary
- 🥄 dash hot pepper sauce

Garnish

- 🥄 fresh rosemary sprigs

Although spatchcock refers generally to a roasting chicken, Rock Cornish game hens are just as good and more convenient to prepare and serve. If they are barbecued, baste them with any remaining marinade and a little olive oil. Serve with a salad and potatoes boulangère.

1 Split the birds in half by cutting down one side of the backbone. Open the birds out and turn them over.

2 Rub them with the lemon juice and olive oil. Place in a shallow heatproof dish.

3 In a bowl, mix together the lemon rind, shallot, garlic, peppercorns, coriander, juniper berries, and allspice. Press the mixture over the birds.

4 Tuck small pieces of rosemary in around the wing and leg joints.

5 Cover and let sit for 2 hours or refrigerate for 8 hours or overnight.

6 Sprinkle the birds with a little hot pepper sauce and cook under a hot broiler for 20–30 minutes, turning and basting occasionally with the juices.

7 Serve, with any remaining pan juices, garnished with sprigs of fresh rosemary.

Matzo Stuffed Spiced Roast Chicken

Serves 4

- 3½–4 lb. chicken
- 1 lemon, cut in half
- salt
- freshly ground black pepper
- 1 tsp. ground cumin
- ¼ tsp. ground turmeric
- 1 tbsp. olive oil
- 1 onion, thinly sliced

Garnish

- fresh parsley sprigs

Matzo Stuffing

- 2–3 matzos, broken into small pieces
- ½ cup chicken soup, stock or water, heated
- 1 tbsp. olive or vegetable oil
- 1 large onion, chopped
- 2 stalks celery, finely chopped
- salt
- freshly ground black pepper
- ½ tsp. ground cumin (optional)
- ¼ tsp. turmeric (optional)
- 1 tbsp. chopped fresh parsley
- 1 egg, beaten

This matzo (unleavened bread) stuffing is delicious enough to use any time. The combination of flavors for the chicken, of cumin and turmeric, typical of Morocco, Tunisia and other Middle Eastern countries, is a great success.

1 Prepare the stuffing. Into a large bowl, place the broken matzos. Pour the hot chicken soup, stock or water over them and let sit until liquid is absorbed.

2 In a large skillet, over medium heat, heat the oil. Add onion and celery and cook until the vegetables begin to soften, 3–4 minutes. Add salt and pepper to taste and sprinkle in the cumin and turmeric. Cook, stirring frequently, until the mixture is golden, 4–5 minutes. Stir in the matzo mixture. Remove from heat and leave to cool. Stir in chopped parsley and beaten egg.

3 Preheat oven to 400°F. Remove any excess fat from the chicken and cavity. Wash under cold running water and pat dry with paper towels. Rub outside of the chicken all over with the lemon half; squeeze other half into cavity. Season chicken with salt and pepper to taste and cumin and turmeric. Rub or brush olive oil over.

4 Spoon stuffing into the bird and close with skewers or toothpicks if necessary. Place sliced onion in a medium roasting pan and lay the chicken on top. Roast, basting with the juices occasionally, for 1¼–1½ hours. Halfway through roasting time, add ½–1 cup water to dissolve juices. Chicken is cooked through when juices run clear when leg is pierced with a knife or skewer.

5 Transfer chicken to carving board and cover loosely with foil. Leave to rest in a warm place for 10–15 minutes.

6 Pour any meat juices and onion into a small saucepan. Heat to boiling and reduce slightly, skimming any foam which comes to the surface. Pour into a gravy boat. Place chicken on serving platter, garnished with parsley. If you like, remove stuffing to a separate bowl for easier serving.

Roast Chicken with Mushroom and Rice Timbales

Serves 4

- 3½ lb. chicken
- ½ lemon
- 1 bayleaf
- ¼ onion, peeled
- sprig of thyme or 1 tsp. mixed herbs
- 2 tbsp. butter

Rice Timbales

- 1 cup mushrooms, washed and sliced
- ¼ cup butter
- 2 tbsp. lemon juice
- generous 1 cup long-grain rice, cooked
- salt and freshly ground black pepper
- 1 tbsp. chopped fresh parsley
- 1 tbsp. grated cheese
- 1 small carrot (optional)

Gravy

- 1 small onion
- 1 bayleaf
- 1¼ cups chicken stock
- 1 tbsp. flour
- 2 tbsp. white wine (optional)

1 Rub over the chicken with the halved lemon. Place the lemon, bayleaf, onion, and herbs inside the cavity of the chicken with a small knob of butter.

2 Rub the remaining butter over the chicken skin and place in a preheated oven at 400°F. Cook for approximately 1 hour 20 minutes or until chicken is tender.

3 Slice the mushrooms. Heat the butter in a skillet and sauté the mushrooms for 3 minutes. Add the lemon juice. Cover the pan and allow all moisture to evaporate without burning the mushrooms.

4 Have the rice already cooked by the absorption method. Mix with salt and pepper, parsley, and grated cheese.

5 Oil small molds or ramekin dishes well. Arrange mushroom slices on the bottom. If you wish, slice some carrot with a cocktail cutter for extra decoration. Blanch the slices in boiling water for 4 minutes, then add to the mushroom design. Mix remaining sliced mushrooms with the rice. Turn the rice into the molds and pack down well.

6 Place the molds in the oven for the last 20 minutes of the chicken's cooking time.

7 Remove the chicken and molds from the oven and allow to stand for 10 minutes before carving and turning out the timbales.

8 To make gravy remove the chicken from the roasting pan and keep warm. Pour off excess fat. If giblets come with the chicken simmer these for at least 30 minutes with an onion, bayleaf, and water for stock. Otherwise use bought chicken stock. Add the flour to the chicken juice in the roasting pan which can be places over a low heat. Whisk the flour and chicken juices together. Add seasoning and, for extra special gravy, white wine. Gradually add the stock and stir until smooth and slightly thickened. Serve in a heated sauce boat.

9 Carve the chicken and serve 1–2 rice timbales with each portion.

Buckwheat Stuffed Roast Chicken

Serves 4-6

- 6 oz. roasted buckwheat
- 2 cups water
- 1 onion, finely chopped
- 2 tbsp. butter
- 1 clove garlic, minced (optional)
- ¼ lb. chicken livers, chopped
- ½ tsp. dried marjoram
- salt and freshly ground black pepper
- 1 egg, beaten
- 3½ lb. chicken

Dill Stuffing

- 1 small onion, finely chopped
- 2 tbsp. butter
- 3 cups fresh white bread crumbs
- 4 tbsp fresh dill, chopped
- 2 eggs
- salt and black pepper

If you would prefer to stuff the chicken with a bread crumb mixture, try the dill stuffing.

1 Place the buckwheat in a sieve and rinse under cold running water. Put the buckwheat in a saucepan and pour in the water. Heat very gently until the water is just about simmering. Remove the pan from the heat, cover and leave for 30 minutes by which time the buckwheat should have absorbed all the water.

2 Cook the onion in the butter for 10 minutes, until soft but not browned. Add the garlic and chicken livers and cook for a further 5 minutes, stirring occasionally, until the pieces of liver are firm. Add this mixture to the buckwheat with the marjoram and seasoning to taste. Stir in the egg to bind, making sure all the ingredients are thoroughly combined.

3 To make a dill stuffing, cook the small, chopped onion in the butter until soft. Mix the onion with the bread crumbs, the chopped fresh dill, salt and freshly ground black pepper, and 2 egg yolks. Whisk the whites until they peak softly, then stir into the stuffing

4 Set the oven at 350°F. Rinse the chicken under cold running water, drain well and pat dry with paper towels. Spoon the stuffing into the body cavity and truss the bird neatly, tying string around the legs and wings. Place in a roasting pan. Roast for 1¼ hours, or until the chicken is golden, crisp and cooked through. Halfway through cooking, pour a little water into the bottom of the roasting pan and keep topping this up as it evaporates.

5 Transfer the cooked chicken to a warmed serving plate. Add a little extra water to the cooking juices, if necessary, and boil the liquid, scraping all the roasting residue off the pan. When the gravy is reduced and flavorsome, check the seasoning and serve a little poured over the chicken.

Barbecue Sauce Roast Chicken

Serves 4

- 3½ lb. chicken
- 1 tbsp. olive oil
- salt and freshly ground black pepper
- 1 medium onion, finely diced
- 4 tbsp. cider or sherry vinegar
- 2 tbsp. tomato paste
- 1 tbsp. clear honey
- 1 tsp. mustard powder
- 1 clove garlic, minced

Garnish

- fresh watercress

This recipe makes a change from the traditional roast. The chicken is coated with a barbecue sauce and roasted in the delicious juices. Alternatively, the sauce can be poured over an equivalent quantity of chicken drumsticks and thighs and cooked for 1 hour instead. Serve with jacket potatoes or boiled rice and seasonal or stir-fried vegetables.

1 Place the chicken in a roasting pan. Rub the oil over the chicken and season with salt and pepper.

2 Roast the chicken for 30 minutes at 400°F.

3 In a screw-top jar or bowl, mix together the remaining ingredients, apart from the garnish. Remove the chicken from the oven and pour the sauce over the bird.

4 Roast for a further 1 hour, basting frequently with the sauce. The skin will turn a rich, dark-brown color.

5 Serve the chicken hot, garnished with fresh sprigs of watercress.

Parmesan Baked Chicken

Serves 4

- 4 boneless half chicken breasts, approx. 5 oz. each
- 2 tbsp. olive oil
- 2 medium onions, finely chopped
- 2 cloves garlic, finely chopped
- 1 stalk celery, chopped
- 14 oz. can chopped tomatoes
- 1 tbsp. tomato paste
- few drops hot pepper sauce
- 1 tsp. chopped fresh basil
- 1 tsp. chopped fresh marjoram
- 1 tsp. sugar
- 2 tbsp. lemon juice
- 1 egg, beaten
- ¼ cup all-purpose flour, seasoned
- 1½ cups grated Mozzarella cheese
- 2 tbsp. grated Parmesan cheese
- salt and freshly ground black pepper

Garnish

- fresh watercress

A topping rich with tomatoes, herbs and Italian cheeses embraces succulent breasts of chicken. Serve with plain new potatoes and fresh spinach.

1 Heat half the oil in a pan and sauté the onions, garlic, and celery until softened. Stir in the tomatoes, paste, hot pepper sauce, herbs, and sugar. Season with salt and pepper. Simmer, uncovered, for 25 – 30 minutes.

2 Sprinkle the skinned chicken breasts with lemon juice. Dip each breast into the egg and then the seasoned flour. Shake off any excess.

3 Heat the remaining oil in a non-stick skillet and sauté the chicken breasts for 5 minutes, turning halfway through, until golden brown. Drain on paper towels.

4 Lay the chicken in an ovenproof dish and cover with half the Mozzarella cheese. Pour over sauce, top with the remaining cheese, and sprinkle with Parmesan.

5 Bake for 25 – 30 minutes at 350°F or until bubbling and golden.

6 Serve, garnished with fresh watercress.

Lime Baked Chicken Pieces

Serves 4

- 4 fresh thyme sprigs
- 1 bayleaf
- 5 oz. No-Cook Mojito
- 2 tbsp. butter or margarine
- ⅓ cup self-rising flour
- 1 tsp. salt
- ½ tsp. freshly ground black pepper

Garnish

- freshly snipped chives (optional)

No-cook Mojito

- 4¼ cups freshly squeezed Seville orange juice (about 20 oranges)
- freshly squeezed juice of 4 limes
- 2 cups olive oil
- 12 cloves garlic, minced
- 1 cup finely chopped onion
- 4 tbsp. dry sherry
- 4 tsp. salt
- 4 tsp. dried marjoram
- 2 tsp. ground cumin
- 4 tbsp. minced fresh ginger root

Good side dishes for this include steamed white rice and coleslaw.

1 Make the No-cook Mojito at least 1 day before use. Stir together Seville orange and lime juices. Blend in oil and then garlic, onion, sherry, salt, marjoram, cumin, and ginger root. Place in a bottle or jar with a tight-fitting lid and refrigerate at least 1 day before use.

2 Stir thyme and bayleaf into Mojito. Marinate chicken in this mixture 2 hours or overnight.

3 Preheat oven to 350°F and butter a roasting pan. Drain marinade and discard. Melt remaining butter. Combine flour, salt and pepper. Dredge chicken pieces in the flour and put them in the oven, drizzled with the melted butter, and bake until well browned, 50–55 minutes.

Southern Stuffed Chicken Thighs

Serves 4

- 1 tbsp. olive oil
- ¼ cup chopped onion
- ¼ cup chopped celery
- 5 oz. uncooked chicken livers, finely chopped
- ¼ tsp. ground ginger
- ¼ tsp. salt
- dash of pepper
- 2 cups soft bread crumbs
- 1 green tart apple, peeled, cored and cut into ¼ inch dice
- ½ cup walnuts, coarsely chopped
- 4–5 tbsp. melted butter
- 3 tbsp. milk
- 8 chicken thighs
- ½ tsp. paprika

Tart apple, walnuts, ginger, celery, and liver make a tasty melange of flavors and textures. The liver is not enough to dominate the stuffing, and it is nicely complemented by the other flavors. This stuffing is a little messy, since there's not enough bread for it to clump together, but that's what allows the other ingredients to assert themselves. Put any leftover stuffing in a small, lightly buttered casserole or baking dish, and add a little melted butter or milk to keep it moist. Cover the dish and bake it during the last 20 minutes while the chicken is cooking, then serve it on the side.

1 In a medium skillet, sauté the onion and celery in the olive oil for 3 minutes. Add the chopped liver. Cook, stirring frequently, until liver is thoroughly browned, about 5 minutes. Add ginger, salt and pepper, and mix well.

2 In a medium bowl, mix bread crumbs, apple and walnuts. Add the liver mixture. Add 2 tbsp. melted butter and enough milk so that stuffing is thoroughly moistened but not mushy.

3 Preheat oven to 350°F. Lightly grease a shallow 9 x 9 inch (or slightly larger) baking dish. Trim excess skin and fat from chicken thighs. Remove bone by cutting thighs almost in half along the bone. Cut out the bone with a sharp knife. Place the boned thighs skin side down and spread out so you have a flat rectangle of meat. Place about 2 tbsp. stuffing along the center of each thigh. Roll up and fasten with wooden toothpicks or tie with string. Push any spilled stuffing back into

roll and place in baking dish, rolled edges up.

4 Mix 2–3 tbsp. melted butter and paprika. Brush butter over thighs. Lightly sprinkle with salt, if desired. Bake at 350°F, occasionally basting with pan juices, until chicken is cooked through, 50–60 minutes.

Baked Chicken with Basil Sauce

Serves 4

- 4 chicken joints, skinned
- 1 cup fresh white bread crumbs
- ¼ cup bacon, rinded, and chopped
- ¼ cup freshly grated Parmesan cheese
- 1 tbsp. parsley, chopped
- 2 cloves garlic, finely chopped
- ½ tsp. mustard powder
- 2 tsp. Worcestershire sauce
- salt and freshly ground black pepper
- 2 tbsp. butter
- 1 tbsp. olive oil

Basil Sauce
- 4 tbsp. olive oil
- 4 tbsp. white wine vinegar
- 1 clove garlic, finely chopped
- 2 oz. fresh basil leaves, finely chopped
- ½ cup fromage frais or natural yogurt

- 1 tsp. cornstarch
- 1 tsp. water
- salt and freshly ground black pepper

Garnish
- fresh basil leaves

Fresh basil is vital for this flavorsome dish and really has no substitute. Accompany with fresh string or snap beans.

1 Place the chicken joints in a shallow baking dish.

2 In a bowl, mix together the bread crumbs, bacon, cheese, parsley, garlic, and mustard powder. Sprinkle on the Worcestershire sauce and season to taste.

3 Press the crumb mixture on top of each chicken joint. Dot with small pieces of butter and drizzle on the oil.

4 Cook for 35–40 minutes at 375°F or until the chicken is tender. (Cover the joints with foil if they get too brown.)

5 Meanwhile, make the Basil Sauce. Combine the oil, vinegar, garlic, and basil leaves in a saucepan. Bring to a boil, then immediately reduce heat to a simmer.

6 Stir in the fromage frais and the cornstarch, blended with the water. Stir until heated through and thickened. Season to taste.

7 Transfer the baked chicken to a warm serving plate and pour the sauce over the center of the joints. Garnish with fresh basil leaves.

Chicken Jurassienne

Serves 4

- 4 boneless half chicken breasts, approx. 5 oz. each, skinned
- ½ cup all-purpose flour
- 2 dashes grated nutmeg
- salt and freshly ground black pepper
- 2 eggs, lightly beaten
- 1½ cups fresh bread crumbs
- scant ⅓ cup Gruyère cheese, finely grated
- 4 tbsp. sunflower oil
- 1 lemon, sliced, to garnish

Garnish
- 1 lemon, sliced,

Although this recipe uses whole chicken breasts, you can, if you prefer, cut the chicken into goujons (wide strips) before crumbing them. Serve accompanied with mixed salad.

1 Slightly flatten the chicken breasts between 2 sheets of dampened wax paper.

2 Mix together the flour, nutmeg, and salt and pepper and thoroughly coat the chicken breasts.

3 Dip the floured chicken breasts in the beaten egg, then into a mixture of bread crumbs and cheese, pressing the crumbs well against the chicken flesh.

4 Place on a lightly oiled baking sheet. Drizzle the oil over the breasts. Cook for 30 minutes at 400°F or until golden brown and crisp.

5 Serve hot, garnished with lemon slices.

Muscat Baked Almond Chicken

Serves 6

- 4½ lb. chicken
- salt and freshly ground pepper
- ½ tsp. cinnamon
- large dash nutmeg
- fresh lemon thyme
- fresh marjoram
- 1½ cups muscat grapes, skinned, seeded and halved
- 1 cup sweet muscat wine
- 1 tbsp. butter
- 3 tbsp. sliced blanched almonds
- ⅓ cup ground almonds
- salt and freshly ground pepper
- ⅔ cup light cream
- 2 egg yolks

This dish is made with the sweet white-green grapes that have been grown around Cyprus and the Levant since Crusader times. Both a wine-making and a dessert grape, the muscat gives a pungent flavor and aroma to this recipe, which has its roots in a centuries-old tradition of using ground almonds as a thickening agent. In Lebanon, the herbs used would be wild – the marjoram, in particular, of a type found only in the eastern Mediterranean.

1 Wash and pat dry the chicken, rub it all over with salt and pepper to taste, the cinnamon, and the nutmeg. Take 2–3 sprigs of lemon thyme and the same of marjoram and put them inside the chicken. Place it in a casserole, stuff with half the grapes and pour over the wine. Cover and cook the chicken in a preheated 400°F oven for 1½ hours.

2 Remove the chicken from the oven and transfer it to a warm serving platter. Remove the grapes and herbs from the cavity, joint the chicken and cover it with foil to keep it warm.

3 In a small saucepan, melt the butter and sauté the sliced almonds for a few minutes until just colored. Remove with a slotted spoon and set aside. Skim the fat from the chicken cooking juices in the casserole and strain them into the saucepan. Heat the juices gently until very hot, but not boiling, and stir in the remaining grapes and the ground almonds. Allow to cook for a few minutes to combine.

4 In a small bowl beat the cream and egg yolks together lightly. Take a spoonful of the hot chicken stock and stir it into the egg. Remove the saucepan from the heat and stir in the egg mixture; the sauce should thicken as you stir.

5 Pour some of the sauce over the jointed chicken and sprinkle it with the toasted almonds. Pour the remainder into a sauceboat to be served with pilau rice.

Orange Glazed Chicken Wings

Serves 4

Glaze
- 2 tbsp. white wine
- grated rind 1 orange
- 6 tbsp. orange juice
- 1 tbsp. lemon juice
- 5 tbsp. honey or stem ginger syrup
- ½ tsp. ground cinnamon
- 1 tsp. ground ginger
- 1 tsp. black peppercorns, crushed
- 1 tsp. coriander seeds, crushed
- 12 fresh chicken wings

Garnish
- rind of 1 orange, julienned strips
- fresh orange segments
- fresh mint

1 Mix all the glaze ingredients together in a large bowl. Add the chicken wings, cover and marinate for at least 4 hours, preferably overnight, in the refrigerator.

2 Line a small roasting pan with a double layer of foil. Pour in the chicken wings and glaze. Arrange the wings so they are outer side uppermost.

3 Bake for 50–60 minutes at 375°F, basting regularly with the glaze. If the glaze is still quite liquid at the end of the cooking time, pour it off into a small pan and boil rapidly until it reduces and thickens. Spoon this back over the wings.

4 Serve the chicken wings hot or cold, garnished with julienne strips of orange rind, orange segments, and fresh mint.

Chicken Kiev

Serves 8-10

- ½ cup olive oil
- 6 sheets of filo pastry, thawed if frozen
- 2 half chicken breasts, skinned, boned and cut into small pieces
- 1 bunch of scallions, chopped
- 3 tbsp. chopped fresh dill
- 2 celery stalks, finely chopped
- salt and freshly ground black pepper, to taste
- 2 tsp. dried thyme
- 1 tsp. dried mint
- ½ tsp. dried marjoram
- ½ tsp. dried tarragon
- 1½ cups crumbled feta cheese

Serves 4

- ½ cup unsalted butter
- grated rind ½ lemon
- 1 tsp. lemon juice
- 1 clove garlic, finely chopped
- 2 tbsp. freshly chopped parsley or chervil
- dash grated nutmeg
- 4 boneless half chicken breasts, approx. 6 oz. each

Coating

- ¼ cup all-purpose seasoned flour
- 3 cups fresh white bread crumbs
- 1 large egg, beaten
- 4 tbsp. vegetable oil

Garnish

- fresh parsley or chervil

Traditionally, this sinful but classic Russian dish used part-boned chicken fillets, but boneless chicken breasts are perhaps more convenient and economical. However, there is no escaping the buttery garlicky filling which oozes calories, so, as a compromise, these kievs are baked in the oven, rather than deep fried.

1 To make the filling, cream together the first six ingredients. Shape the savory butter into a rectangle, wrap in foil and chill until hard.

2 Remove the skins from the chicken. Cut a small pocket in the side of each breast. Gently beat the breasts between 2 sheets of wax paper to flatten slightly.

3 Cut the hard butter into 4 fingers and tuck each one into a breast pocket. Fold the cut edge over neatly and secure, if necessary, with a toothpick.

4 Dust the chicken with the lightly seasoned flour, then dip in the beaten egg and coat with the bread crumbs, pressing them on firmly. Refrigerate for an hour.

5 Place the kievs on a lightly oiled baking sheet. Drizzle over the oil and cook for 35–40 minutes at 375°F or until the coating is golden brown and crisp. Serve immediately, garnished with chopped parsley or chervil.

Serves 4

- 1 tsp. cornstarch
- grated rind ½ lemon
- 3 tbsp. natural yogurt
- 3 cardamom pods, seeds only, crushed
- ½ tsp. coriander seeds, crushed
- 1 tbsp. freshly chopped chervil
- 2 tsp. freshly chopped tarragon
- 2 tsp. Dijon-style mustard
- salt and freshly ground black pepper
- 4 boneless half chicken breasts, approx. 6 oz., skinned

Garnish

- lemon slices
- fresh chervil

Herb, Cheese and Chicken Pie

- 🍲 *2 tbsp. grated fresh Parmesan cheese*
- 🍲 *2 eggs, lightly beaten*
- 🍲 *½ tsp. ouzo (optional)*
- 🍲 *1 egg yolk, beaten, to glaze*

This pie is perfect fare for summertime entertaining outside. Delicious hot or cold, it's easy to make and always looks impressive.

1 Preheat the oven to 350°F. Grease a 10 inch pie dish with some of the olive oil. Lay the filo pastry out on the work surface and cover with a slightly damp cloth to prevent it from drying out.

2 Place the chicken breasts in a large mixing bowl with the scallions, dill, celery, salt and freshly ground black pepper, and herbs. Scatter in the crumbled feta and the grated cheese and mix thoroughly to combine. Add the beaten eggs, ouzo, if using, 2 tbsp. olive oil and mix.

3 Separate one sheet of filo pastry from the rest and lay it on the work surface, keeping the remaining sheets covered with the cloth. Brush the separated sheet with some of the olive oil, then lay another sheet of filo pastry on top. Brush with oil and repeat with a third layer of pastry. Brush again with olive oil, then lay the oiled sheets in the base of the pie dish, allowing the excess pastry to hang over the edges of the plate.

4 Spoon the chicken mixture into the lined pie dish and spread it out evenly. Repeat the brushing and layering process with the remaining sheets of pastry, then lay them on top of the chicken filling.

5 Roll the edges of the filo pastry together to firmly seal in the filling and make a few small incisions in the top of the pie to allow the steam to escape during cooking. Brush with the beaten egg yolk to glaze and bake for 45–50 minutes or until the pastry is crisp and the chicken is cooked through. Serve warm or cold, cut into slices.

Fragrant Chicken Parcels

These parcels, containing fresh herbs, yogurt and succulent chicken, can be cooked in the oven, over a steamer or in with the barbecue charcoals. Whichever method is chosen, the result is deliciously aromatic. Accompany with new potatoes and string or snap beans.

1 In a shallow dish, blend together the first nine ingredients. Make a couple of slashes in the chicken breasts, then coat the chicken with the sauce. Leave in the dish, cover and marinate for 2–3 hours in a cool place.

2 Place each breast in the center of a large piece of foil. Spoon over any remaining marinade. Wrap the foil up around the chicken, making sure you seal it well.

3 Cook for 20–25 minutes at 375°F or until the chicken is tender. Serve the

chicken in the foil parcels, opened up and garnish it with lemon slices and fresh chervil.

Louisiana Chicken Pot Pie with Cornmeal Crust

Serves 6

- 5 tbsp. butter, divided
- 1 small onion, chopped
- 3 cups mushrooms, sliced
- 4 tbsp. flour
- ½ cup heavy cream
- 1 tsp. salt
- ¼ tsp. pepper
- dash cayenne
- 1–1¼ lb. cooked chicken, cubed

Crust

- 1 cup flour
- 1 cup cornmeal
- 1 tbsp. sugar
- 1 tbsp. baking powder
- 1 tsp. salt
- 1 egg, lightly beaten with fork
- 1 cup milk
- 4 tbsp. butter

This version of old-fashioned chicken pot pie is made with a comforting mixture of chicken and mushrooms as its main ingredients. If you prefer, you can substitute peas and carrots for part of the mushrooms. Some people also like to add a little diced ham to the filling.

1 Sauté the onion and mushrooms in 3 tbsp. butter for 6–8 minutes, until the mushrooms are very tender.

2 In a small saucepan, make a light roux of the remaining butter and flour. Heat but do not brown the butter, then add the flour. Cook over low heat, stirring constantly, until the roux is a tan color. While the roux is cooking, bring the chicken stock to a boil. When the roux is done, add a little of the stock to the roux, then gradually stir in the rest. Add the cream, the mushrooms, seasonings, and the chicken. Mix well. Pour into a 10 inch deep-dish pie pan.

3 Mix the flour, cornmeal, sugar, baking powder, and salt in a medium bowl. In a small bowl, combine the egg, milk, and melted butter. Pour the liquid ingredients into the dry ingredients and stir until the flour is evenly moistened. Spoon the mixture over the top of the chicken filling.

4 Bake until the crust is golden brown, about 40 minutes.

Caribbean Chicken Casserole

Serves 6

- 3½ lb. chicken, cut into 2 inch pieces
- 1 tsp. salt
- 1 tsp. freshly ground black pepper
- 2 garlic cloves
- ¼ tsp. chopped fresh thyme
- 2 tsp. vinegar
- 1 bayleaf

- 2 tbsp. vegetable oil
- 1 medium tomato, chopped
- 2 stalks celery, chopped
- 2 carrots, diced
- ¼ cabbage, shredded
- 4 potatoes, chopped
- 6 oz. green beans, cleaned

1 Wash the chicken. Marinate the pieces in a bowl with the salt, pepper, garlic, thyme, bayleaf, and vinegar for 5 hours.

2 Heat the oil in a large saucepan, then add the tomatoes and chicken pieces. Cover with cold water, bring it to a boil, then lower the heat and simmer, covered, for 30 minutes or until the chicken is almost cooked and the liquid has reduced.

3 Add the onion and the other vegetables, and cook until they are tender but crisp.

4 Serve immediately with fresh bread or boiled rice and hot pepper sauce.

Farmyard Chicken with Olives

Serves 4

- 2¼ lb. corn fed chicken, quartered and backbone freed
- 2 onions, chopped
- 2 tbsp. olive oil
- 3 garlic cloves, chopped
- salt and freshly ground black pepper
- 24 green olives
- ¼ cup fino sherry or Montilla
- 2 bayleaves

This is a favorite dish because sherry and olives set off the flavor of chicken so well. It is good served hot from the casserole, but better still jellied. Cutting up the chicken first means it takes less time to cook and improves the quality of the sauce, because it reduces the amount of liquid. In Spain it is served with bread, but rice (hot or cold) could be used.

1 Fry the onions in the oil in a casserole, adding the garlic when they soften. Salt and pepper the chicken portions and pack these neatly into the pan, with the backbone, putting the olives in the spaces.

Add the fino and bayleaves and pour in water to almost cover, (about 1½ cups). Simmer, covered, for 30—35 minutes.

2 Spoon the chicken from the casserole, allow to cool for a few minutes. Remove the bones and skin. Return these to the liquid and boil for a further 10 minutes. Check the seasonings.

3 Meanwhile split the cooked chicken into large pieces, arrange them in a shallow dish and distribute the olives. Strain the juices into a bowl and skim off all fat. Pour over the chicken and chill until set.

Tomato and Chicken Casserole

Serves 4-6

- ¼ cup olive oil
- 3½ lb. prepared chicken, cut into portions
- flour, for dredging
- 2 large red onions, sliced
- 2 x 14 oz. cans chopped tomatoes
- 3 cloves garlic cloves, minced
- salt and freshly ground black pepper, to taste
- ⅓ cup boiling water
- 2 tbsp. red wine vinegar

Garnish

- chopped fresh parsley

1 Preheat the oven to 375°F. Heat the oil in a large, flameproof casserole. Place the chicken portions on a chopping board and dredge all over with flour. Place in the casserole and cook for about 5 minutes, or until evenly browned, turning the portions as they cook. Using a slotted spoon, transfer the chicken portions to a plate and set aside.

2 Add the onion to the casserole and cook for 3 minutes, or until softened. Return the chicken to the casserole, add the chopped tomatoes and garlic and season with salt and freshly ground black pepper. Add the boiling water, cover, and cook in the oven for 45–55 minutes or until the chicken is tender and the sauce has thickened.

3 In the last 5 minutes of cooking time, stir in the red wine vinegar and a little extra boiling water if necessary. Serve sprinkled with chopped fresh parsley.

Nutty Ricardo Chicken Wings

Serves 4

- 12 chicken wings
- salt and freshly ground black pepper to taste
- 2 tbsp. creamy peanut butter
- 2 tbsp. soy sauce
- 1½ tbsp. honey
- ½ tsp. ground cumin
- 1 clove garlic, minced
- ¼–½ tsp. dried hot red-pepper flakes, or ½ fresh or canned jalapeño pepper, seeded and finely minced

Garnish

- ¾ cup finely chopped peanuts
- 3–4 tbsp. finely chopped fresh cilantro

1 Preheat oven to 400°F. In a shallow baking pan lined with foil, season chicken wings with salt and pepper. Bake in middle of oven for 30 minutes, or until they begin to turn brown and become crisp.

2 While chicken wings are baking, in a small saucepan, stir together peanut butter, soya sauce, honey, cumin, garlic, and pepper flakes. Cook over a low heat, stirring until smooth. Brush chicken wings generously with sauce and bake them for 10–15 more minutes. Sprinkle chicken wings immediately with chopped peanuts and cilantro and let them cool slightly before serving.

Rich Tomato Chicken Creole

Serves 6

- 5 half chicken breasts, boned and skinned
- 1 tbsp. flour
- 1 tsp. salt
- ¼ tsp. dried thyme
- ½ tsp. dried marjoram
- ½ tsp. dried basil
- ½ tsp. paprika
- ⅛ tsp. cayenne
- ⅛ tsp. black pepper
- ⅛ tsp. white pepper
- 4 tbsp. vegetable oil, divided
- 1 cup chopped onions
- 1 cup chopped green pepper
- 1 cup chopped celery
- 2 cloves garlic, finely chopped
- 3 cups chicken stock
- 1¼ lb. fresh tomatoes, seeded and chopped
- 8 oz. can tomato sauce
- 1 tsp. sugar
- few drops hot pepper sauce
- salt to taste
- ½ oz. fresh parsley, chopped
- ¼ cup chopped scallions
- 1¼ lb. cooked rice

This Louisiana Creole dish is based on a rich, spicy tomato sauce that is cooked long and slow, then served over rice. The seasoning comes from the chicken, which is cubed, tossed with a spice mixture and sautéed before it is added to the pot. It's also good made with shrimp.

1 Cut the chicken into bite-size cubes. Mix the flour and spices in a small bowl. Sprinkle the spices over the chicken, and toss the chicken so the cubes are evenly covered with spice. Heat 2 tbsp. oil in a skillet. Sauté the chicken until it is lightly browned and cooked through, about 10 minutes. Remove the chicken with a slotted spoon, and set aside.

2 Add the additional oil to the pan, if necessary. Sauté the onion, pepper, celery, and garlic for 5 minutes.

3 In a large saucepan, bring the chicken stock to a boil. Add the chicken, sautéed vegetables, tomatoes, tomato sauce, and sugar. Simmer, covered, for 45 minutes, stirring occasionally. Add hot pepper sauce and salt to taste. Just before serving, stir in the parsley and scallions. Spoon the Creole sauce over rice in bowls and serve.

Creole Chicken Stew with Dumplings

Serves 4

Chicken Stock

- 1 chicken, about 3½ lb., cut in half
- 2 lb. extra chicken necks and backs
- 2 carrots, unpeeled, cut into chunks
- ½ onion, cut into chunks
- 2 stalks celery, including leaves, sliced
- 1 bayleaf
- 1½ tsp. fresh thyme or ½ tsp. dried
- 4 black peppercorns
- 1 tsp. salt

Stew

- 3 tbsp. shortening
- 3 tbsp. all-purpose flour
- 3 cups chopped onion
- 1 large green bell pepper, chopped
- 2 cups chopped celery
- 2 medium tomatoes, seeded and chopped
- 1¼ cups chicken stock (above)
- meat from 1 chicken, cut into strips or bite-sized pieces
- ¼ tsp. dry mustard
- ½ tsp. paprika
- large dash white pepper
- large dash cayenne
- salt to taste
- 2 tbsp. chopped fresh parsley

Dumplings

- 1¼ cups all-purpose flour
- 1½ tsp. baking powder
- ½ tsp. salt
- 1 tsp. dry mustard
- ¼ tsp. cayenne
- 2 eggs, lightly beaten
- ¼ cup milk
- ¼ cup butter, melted
- 2–3 scallions, finely chopped
- 2 tbsp. chopped fresh parsley

This chicken stew in a spicy tomato sauce takes the better part of a day to make, but it makes a hearty dish that is worth the effort. It begins with a chicken stock, made with the chicken that eventually goes into the stew.

1 Put all the chicken stock ingredients into a large stockpot and cover with water. Bring to a boil and skim off the grey-brown foam. Reduce the heat and simmer for about 45 minutes. Remove the chicken halves and let cool briefly so you can handle them. Cut the meat from bones and refrigerate the meat.

2 Return the bones and skin to the stock and continue simmering, uncovered, for a total of about 3 hours. Strain the stock, discarding the bones. You will need 1¼ cups stock for the Creole stew; freeze or refrigerate any remaining stock for future use. Skim any fat from the top of the stock.

3 In a medium, heavy saucepan, make a roux of shortening and flour. Remove from the heat and stir in the stew vegetables. Return to the heat and cook until the vegetables are limp, about 5 minutes.

4 In a deep skillet or large saucepan, bring the chicken stock to a boil. Add the roux and vegetables, 1 large spoonful at a time, whisking after each addition. Add the chicken and seasonings and simmer 30 minutes, uncovered.

5 Meanwhile, prepare the dumplings. Mix the flour, baking powder, and seasonings in a bowl. Combine the eggs, milk, and butter in a second bowl. Pour the liquids into the dry ingredients and stir just until blended. Stir in the scallions and parsley.

6 Drop spoonfuls of dough into the top of a steamer over simmering water. Cover and steam until the dumplings have risen slightly (about 7 minutes).

7 Transfer the dumplings to the top of the stew and cook an additional 5 minutes, uncovered.

Trinidad-style Chicken

Serves 4-6

- 2 tbsp. lime juice
- 1 medium onion, chopped
- 1 large tomato, cut into 8 wedges
- 1 stalk celery, chopped
- 1 tbsp. chopped scallions
- 3 tbsp. minced fresh cilantro
- 1 clove garlic, chopped
- ⅛ tsp. dried thyme, crumbled
- 1 tsp. salt
- ⅛ tsp. freshly ground black pepper
- 1 tbsp. white wine vinegar
- 2 tbsp. Worcestershire sauce
- 1½ –2 lb. chicken, cut into serving pieces
- 2 tbsp. vegetable oil
- 2 tbsp. dark brown sugar
- 2 tbsp. tomato catsup
- 1 cup water
- 2 cups shredded cabbage (optional)

Garnish

- celery leaves (optional)
- lime slices (optional)

1 In a large bowl, combine the lime juice, onion, tomato, celery, scallions, cilantro, garlic, thyme, salt, pepper, vinegar, and Worcestershire sauce. Add the chicken, turning it to coat well, and let marinate in the refrigerator, covered, overnight.

2 In a heavy-based saucepan, heat the oil over medium-high heat until it is hot but not smoking and add the sugar. When the sugar mixture begins to bubble, transfer the chicken in batches to the pan, using a slotted spoon. Reserve the marinade mixture. Cook the chicken, turning it until it is browned well, and transfer it to paper towels to drain. Stir the reserved marinade mixture, tomato catsup, and water into the fat remaining in the saucepan and return the chicken to the pan. Bring the mixture to a boil and simmer it, covered, stirring occasionally, for 30 minutes. Add the shredded cabbage, if using, and simmer for 15–20 minutes until the thickest pieces of chicken are done. Garnish with celery leaves or lime slices if desired.

Calypso Chicken

Serves 6

- 3 lb. chicken, cut into 2 inch pieces
- ½ lemon
- 2 tsp. salt
- freshly ground black pepper
- 2 cloves garlic
- 1 tbsp. vinegar
- ¼ tsp. chopped fresh thyme
- 2 tbsp. butter or margarine
- 2 tsp. brown sugar
- oil for frying
- 2 cups cashew nuts
- 1 cup mushrooms, sliced
- 3 onions, chopped
- 6 slices fresh root ginger
- 1 tbsp. all-purpose flour

1 Wash the chicken in cold running water, rubbing with the lemon. Season with the salt, pepper, one of the cloves of garlic, crushed, plus the vinegar and thyme. Let marinate for about 3 hours.

2 In a large saucepan, melt the butter or margarine, then add the sugar. When it is bubbling, add the chicken and brown the pieces.

3 Meanwhile, in a skillet, heat some oil. Fry half the cashews, then set them aside. In the same pan, fry together the remaining clove of garlic, crushed, the mushrooms, the other half of the cashews, onions and ginger. Add ¼ cup water, and pour the mixture into the large saucepan over the chicken. Cook for 25 minutes or until the chicken is cooked.

4 Thicken with the flour mixed with some warm water and stirred into the chicken mixture. Cook for 3 more minutes, then sprinkle with the remaining fried cashews.

5 Serve with boiled rice.

Lebanese Chicken with Apricots and Olives

Serves 4-6

- ❧ 3½ lb. skinned, boned and cubed chicken
- ❧ 5 cloves garlic, minced
- ❧ 1 cup chopped ready-to-eat dried apricots
- ❧ ¼ cup black Greek olives
- ❧ ½ tsp. grated orange peel
- ❧ 5 tbsp. orange juice
- ❧ 2 tbsp. lemon juice or white wine vinegar
- ❧ ½ cup arak (anise-based Lebanese liqueur) or ouzo
- ❧ 2 tbsp. fresh fennel leaves
- ❧ 1½ tbsp. olive oil
- ❧ ⅔ cup light brown sugar

This savory combination owes more to the Israeli taste than to classic Lebanese cuisine. Israel is Europe's richest source of dried fruits, and they make a frequent appearance in the meat stews and desserts of that country. However, taste cannot be confined by national borders, and dishes like this one have become adapted to include specialties such as *arak* or ouzo.

❶ Preheat the oven to 400°F.

❷ Combine all the ingredients in a large bowl and stir carefully to mix well. Cover and chill overnight.

❸ Transfer the chicken pieces to a baking sheet and pour over the marinade, including the olives and apricots. Sprinkle over the sugar. Bake for about 30 minutes, turning once or twice.

❹ Remove the chicken pieces to a serving platter, and arrange the olives and apricots over and around them. Strain the cooking juices into a saucepan, and reduce over high heat to about half. Pour the sauce over the chicken. Serve warm or cold.

Country Chicken Hotpot

Serves 4

- 4 medium-sized potatoes
- 2 large carrots, peeled and chopped
- 3 stalks celery, chopped
- 1½ cups shredded green cabbage
- 4 chicken legs, approx. 6 oz. each
- ¼ cup seasoned flour
- 2 tbsp. vegetable oil
- 1 tbsp. chopped fresh thyme
- salt and freshly ground black pepper
- 1¼ cups beef stock
- ⅔ cup Guinness or dark beer
- 1 tbsp. dark soft brown sugar
- 1 egg, beaten

Garnish

- chopped fresh thyme

Reminiscent of the Irish hot pot, made even more authentic by addition of some Irish stout!

1 Peel the potatoes; cut two of the potatoes into thin slices, and chop the other two.

2 Mix the chopped potato with the carrot, celery, and cabbage.

3 Dust the chicken legs with seasoned flour. Heat the oil in a large pan and sauté the chicken legs until lightly golden on all sides. Add thyme, and salt and pepper to taste.

4 Place half of the mixed vegetables in the base of a deep casserole. Top with the chicken legs and then the remaining vegetables.

5 Mix the stock , Guinness or beer, and brown sugar together and pour over the contents of the casserole.

6 Overlap the potato slices in concentric circles on top of the vegetables and chicken. Brush with a little oil.

7 Cover with a piece of lightly oiled foil and cook at 350°F for 1 hour.

8 Remove the foil. Brush the potato crust with the beaten egg. Return to the oven for a further 35–40 minutes. Serve sprinkled with chopped thyme.

Armenian-style Chicken and Garbanzo Stew

Serves 6

- 🍃 *4 threads saffron*
- 🍃 *½ cup hot water*
- 🍃 *10 cloves garlic, minced*
- 🍃 *2 fresh thin medium-hot chiles, seeded and chopped*
- 🍃 *4 tbsp. vegetable or sunflower oil*
- 🍃 *3 lb. chicken breasts and thighs, washed and dried*
- 🍃 *salt and freshly ground black pepper*
- 🍃 *2 tbsp. ground coriander*
- 🍃 *1 tsp. dried marjoram*
- 🍃 *2 x 14 oz. cans tomatoes, drained*
- 🍃 *2 cups water*
- 🍃 *1¼ lb. can garbanzos, drained*
- 🍃 *2 tbsp. lemon juice*

The Armenians have a spicy condiment sold as Aintab Red Pepper here in the West. Since it is difficult to find, two thin medium-hot red chiles have been substituted here.

1 Soak the saffron in hot water for 10 minutes. Place the saffron and liquid, garlic, and chiles in a blender or food processor. Process until finely chopped and set aside.

2 Heat the oil in a casserole over medium-hot heat. Season the chicken to taste, and sauté in batches until lightly browned. Remove to a plate and keep warm.

3 Reduce the heat and add the crushed garlic. Stir with a wooden spoon for 2 minutes, then add the ground coriander and marjoram. Stir for a further 2 minutes, then add the tomatoes. Break them up with the spoon while cooking for 3 minutes, then add the water. Add the chicken pieces and spoon the sauce over them. Bring to a boil, cover, and simmer over low heat for 20 minutes.

4 Add the garbanzos and continue to cook, covered, for a further 15 minutes. Remove the lid, stir in the lemon juice, and increase the heat. Boil for 5 minutes to reduce the sauce. Serve immediately.

Sauternes and Cinnamon Chicken

Serves 4

- 4 boneless half chicken breasts, approx. 6 oz. each, skinned
- 2 tbsp. sunflower oil
- 1 medium onion, finely chopped
- 1 clove garlic, minced
- 3 inch piece of cinnamon stick, bruised
- 1¼ cups Sauternes (or similar sweet white wine)
- salt and freshly ground black pepper
- 2 egg yolks
- ⅔ cup low fat natural yogurt or fromage frais

Garnish

- 12 pickling onions
- 2 tbsp. butter
- 1 tbsp. soft brown sugar

- crumbled or flaked cinnamon stick
- fresh cilantro

A new and delicious combination of chicken and cinnamon to grace any dinner party.

1 Heat the oil in a large pan and sauté the chicken breasts until evenly colored on all sides. Remove and keep warm.

2 Add the onion, garlic, and bruised cinnamon stick to the pan and cook for a few minutes or until the onions are softened.

3 Return the chicken to the pan, add the Sauternes and salt and pepper, to taste. Cover and simmer gently for 20—25 minutes until the chicken is tender.

4 Meanwhile toss the baby onions in the butter until translucent and well glazed.

5 Transfer the chicken to a serving plate and keep warm. Discard cinnamon stick. Blend the cooking juices until smooth. Return to a clean pan.

6 Beat the egg yolks with the yogurt and stir into the sauce. Heat through gently, stirring continuously.

7 Spoon the sauce over the cooked chicken breasts and garnish with the crumbled cinnamon stick, glazed pickling onions, reheated if necessary, and sprigs of fresh cilantro.

Chicken Provençal

Serves 4

- 4 chicken legs or half breasts, approx. 6 oz. each
- 8 sprigs thyme
- 4 slices lean bacon, rinded
- 1 tbsp. vegetable oil
- 1 large onion, chopped
- 2 cloves garlic, finely chopped
- 8 tomatoes, skinned, seeded and shredded
- 1 tsp. tomato paste
- 1 tsp. all-purpose flour
- 1¼ cups dry white wine
- salt and freshly ground black pepper

Garnish

- ½ inch slices French bread, toasted
- 2 tbsp. chopped fresh parsley

Tomatoes, thyme, and garlic provide a taste of Provençe. Omit the bacon slices, if you wish – but you may need to add extra oil. Add the thyme sprigs directly to the pan. The dish is delicious with plain potatoes and string or snap beans.

1 Skin the chicken joints. Lay a sprig of thyme on the top and underside of each joint and wrap a piece of bacon around it, securing with a toothpick.

2 Heat the oil in a pan and sauté the chicken until the joints and bacon are a deep golden color. Remove and put to one side.

3 Add the onion and garlic to the pan and cook until softened. Stir in the tomatoes and paste and cook for a further minute.

4 Sprinkle the flour over the onion mixture and stir well until blended. Gradually pour in the wine. Bring to a boil, stirring, until slightly thickened. Reduce heat. Season to taste.

5 Return the chicken joints to the pan, cover, and simmer for 45 minutes or until the chicken is tender.

6 Transfer the chicken to a warm serving dish (remove the toothpicks). Bring the sauce to a boil and let bubble until it is reduced to the consistency of light cream.

7 Pour the sauce over the chicken. Garnish with freshly toasted French bread and a generous sprinkling of the chopped parsley.

Pernod Flamed Chicken Thighs

Serves 4

- 8–12 chicken thighs (depending on size)
- 2 tbsp. vegetable oil
- 2 shallots or 1 small sweet onion, finely chopped
- 4 tbsp. water
- 6 tbsp. Pernod
- salt and freshly ground black pepper

Garnish

- chopped fresh parsley

A quick and easy standby, good enough on its own with crusty brown bread, or served with fresh vegetables.

1 Heat the oil in a large pan. Cook the chicken for 8 minutes, browning all sides. Reduce the heat, add the shallots, or onion, and water. Cover the pan and simmer gently for 30–35 minutes or until the chicken is tender.

2 Remove the lid, increase the heat and pour in the Pernod. Set alight with a match, and turn off the heat. When the flames die down, scrape up any sediment from the bottom of the pan.

3 Remove the chicken portions to a warm serving dish. Season the remaining juices with salt and pepper and bring to a boil. Spoon over the chicken and serve, garnished with a sprinkling of parsley.

Chicken Marengo

Serves 4

- 3 tbsp. olive oil
- 4 chicken thighs, skinned
- 4 chicken drumsticks, skinned
- 1 large onion, chopped
- 2 cloves garlic, chopped
- ¼ cup all-purpose flour
- ⅔ cup chicken stock
- 1¼ cups Marsala or medium white wine
- 6 tomatoes, skinned and chopped
- 1 tbsp. tomato paste
- 2 cups button mushrooms, halved
- 1 tbsp. chopped fresh basil
- 1 tbsp. brandy
- salt and freshly ground black pepper

Garnish

- 8 cooked shrimps
- fresh basil leaves

This classic dish dates back to 1800 when, according to legend, Napoleon's chef created this recipe in celebration of their victory at the Battle of Marengo. Ingredients then included freshwater crawfish substituted in this version with a garnish of cooked shrimp. Accompany with new potatoes or noodles.

1 Heat the oil and sauté the chicken portions until golden all over. Add the onions and garlic and continue cooking until the onion softens.

2 Sprinkle over the flour, and cook, stirring, until the fat is absorbed and the flour turns a deep golden brown.

3 Gradually blend in the stock and Marsala. Bring to a boil, then reduce the heat to a simmer and cook, covered, for 10 minutes.

4 Stir in the tomatoes, paste, mushrooms, basil, and brandy. Season to taste and simmer, uncovered, for a further 40 minutes.

5 Remove the saucepan lid for the last 20 minutes to allow the sauce to reduce. Stir occasionally to prevent the sauce sticking.

6 Serve, garnished with fresh cooked shrimp and fresh basil leaves.

Chicken Livers in Madeira Sauce

Serves 4-6

- 1½ lb. chicken livers
- milk
- 4 tbsp. butter
- 1 onion, sliced
- salt and freshly ground black pepper
- 2 cups flour
- ¾ cup chicken stock
- ½ cup Madeira
- ½ cup sour cream

Garnish

- fresh parsley, finely chopped

This recipe is so delicious – and so rich – that it would make an elegant and inexpensive main course. Spoon it over rice or, more authentically, use to fill dinner-sized puff-pastry shells.

1 Immerse the chicken livers in milk to just cover, and soak for 2 hours. Drain thoroughly, and discard the milk.

2 Melt the butter over medium heat, and sauté the onion until softened. Dip the chicken livers in seasoned flour, and add to the onions. Fry gently until just colored, about 5 minutes. Stir in the stock and the Madeira, cover, and simmer for about 10 minutes, or until the livers are tender. Season the sauce to taste.

3 Transfer the livers to a bowl; boil the sauce until it is well reduced. Turn down the heat and whisk in the sour cream, a little at a time. Return the livers to the pan, spoon the sauce over, and heat through gently. Serve immediately, sprinkled with fresh parsley.

Chicken Chasseur

Serves 4

- 3 lb. chicken
- 1 tbsp. vegetable oil
- 1 cup button mushrooms, halved
- 2 shallots or 1 small sweet onion, finely chopped
- 2 tbsp. all-purpose flour
- 2 tbsp. brandy
- ½ cup dry white wine
- 2 tsp. tomato paste
- 1¼ cups chicken stock
- 1 tsp. chopped fresh tarragon
- 1 tsp. chopped fresh chervil
- salt and freshly ground black pepper

Garnish

- freshly chopped parsley
- toasted bread croûtes

Any recipe which has "Chasseur" in its title will almost certainly include mushrooms, shallots, and white wine in the list of ingredients. This special chicken dish is easy to prepare, can be made in advance and reheated successfully. Accompany with fresh vegetables.

1 Joint the chicken into 8 pieces.

2 Heat the oil in a large pan and cook the chicken leg joints gently for 6 minutes, turning once. Then add the wings and breast and sauté slowly until golden brown all over. Remove, cover and keep warm.

3 Add the shallots or onion to the pan and cook for 1–2 minutes or until softened and golden. Stir in the mushrooms and continue to cook until they become golden. (Add a little more oil if necessary.)

4 Sprinkle on the flour and blend into the mixture. Gradually stir in the brandy, wine and tomato paste and stock, until the mixture is smooth and thickened. Season to taste.

5 Return the chicken joints to the pan. Sprinkle in the tarragon and chervil and simmer, half covered, for 10–15 minutes.

6 Serve, garnished with the croûtes and a sprinkling of parsley.

Apple and Chicken Parcels with Calabrese

Serves 4

- 4 boneless half chicken breasts, each approx. 7 oz., skinned
- 2 crisp eating apples
- 8 slices smoked bacon, derinded
- 1 tbsp. sunflower oil
- 1 clove garlic, minced
- 1¼ cups apple juice (preferably English)
- 1½ lb. calabrese or broccoli, washed and trimmed
- 2 tbsp. butter
- ½ cup flaked almonds
- 1 tsp. cornstarch
- 1 tbsp. water
- salt and freshly ground black pepper

Garnish

- parsley, freshly chopped

1 Place each chicken breast between a sheet of wax paper and flatten with a rolling pin.

2 Peel, core and slice one apple. Divide the slices between the centers of each chicken breast and roll up. Wrap each breast with 2 slices bacon, securing with wooden toothpicks to make 4 parcels.

3 Heat the oil and garlic in a pan, and add the chicken parcels. Cook gently for 10 minutes, browning on all sides.

4 Peel and core the remaining apple and cut across to form rings. Place one ring on top of each parcel, add the apple juice. Cover and simmer gently for 15 minutes.

5 Cook the calabrese in boiling salted water for 10 minutes or until tender.

6 Meanwhile, melt the butter in a large skillet, add the almonds and cook gently, stirring continuously until browned.

7 Drain the calabrese, transfer to a warm serving dish and sprinkle with the almonds.

8 Remove the chicken to a warm serving dish. Blend the cornstarch with the water and add to the pan juices. Stir and cook until thickened.

9 Spoon the sauce over each parcel and garnish with chopped parsley. Serve the calabrese separately.

Broccoli and Cashew Nuts with Chicken

Serves 4

- 🍃 1 tbsp. cornstarch
- 🍃 6 tbsp. dry sherry
- 🍃 6 tbsp. soy sauce
- 🍃 ½ cup chicken stock
- 🍃 1 tsp. sesame oil
- 🍃 3 tbsp. sunflower or peanut oil
- 🍃 2 large boneless half chicken breasts, skinned and cut into thin strips
- 🍃 6 tbsp. unsalted cashew nuts
- 🍃 ¼ lb. broccoli florets, broken into small pieces
- 🍃 7 oz. can bamboo shoots, drained and sliced
- 🍃 6 scallions, sliced diagonally

1 Blend the cornstarch to a smooth thin paste with the sherry, soy sauce, and stock, then set the mixture aside.

2 Heat the sesame and sunflower or peanut oil, then stir-fry the chicken and cashew nuts until the chicken is golden and cooked, and the nuts are lightly browned.

3 Add the broccoli, bamboo shoots, and scallions and stir-fry for 3–4 minutes, until the broccoli is lightly cooked.

4 Stir the cornstarch mixture, then pour it into the pan and stir over medium heat until the sauce boils. Allow it to boil for a minute or so, stirring all the time, so that all the ingredients are coated in a lightly thickened sauce. Serve at once.

Poached Chicken with Almond and Horseradish Sauce

Serves 4

- 🍃 4½ lb. boiling chicken
- 🍃 1 carrot, peeled and chopped
- 🍃 1 onion, peeled
- 🍃 1 bayleaf
- 🍃 8 peppercorns
- 🍃 4 cloves
- 🍃 3 tbsp. butter
- 🍃 ⅓ cup all-purpose flour
- 🍃 4 tbsp. horseradish relish
- 🍃 ½ cup blanched almonds, coarsely chopped
- 🍃 1 tbsp. chopped fresh parsley
- 🍃 6 tbsp. fromage frais
- 🍃 salt and freshly ground black pepper

Garnish

- 🍃 ¼ cup flaked almonds

The addition of horseradish adds a pungent flavor to this chicken dish; yet it may have your guests trying to identify the "mystery ingredient."

1 Place the chicken in a large pan. Add the carrot, onion, bayleaf, peppercorns, and cloves. Pour on enough cold water to cover the chicken. Gradually bring to a boil, then reduce heat and simmer, covered, for 2–2½ hours or until tender.

2 Remove the chicken, skin and joint it and keep warm in a covered serving dish. Strain off and reserve 2½ cups of the stock for the sauce.

3 Melt the butter in a pan and blend in the flour. Cook for a minute. Remove from the heat and gradually blend in the stock. Return to the heat and stir, until thickened.

4 Stir in the horseradish relish, chopped almonds, and parsley. Simmer for 5 minutes. Add the fromage frais and warm through. Season.

5 Spoon the sauce over the chicken and garnish with the flaked almonds. Serve immediately, accompanied with fresh garden vegetables.

Tarragon Chicken

Serves 4

- ❧ 3½ lb. chicken, jointed
- ❧ juice of ½ lemon
- ❧ 2 tbsp. sunflower oil
- ❧ 1 onion, quartered
- ❧ 1 stalk celery, chopped
- ❧ 1 carrot, peeled and chopped
- ❧ 1 sprig fresh tarragon
- ❧ 6 black peppercorns
- ❧ salt

Sauce

- ❧ 1 tbsp. butter
- ❧ 1 tbsp. sunflower oil
- ❧ 1 clove garlic, finely chopped
- ❧ 2 tbsp. chopped fresh tarragon
- ❧ 1 tsp. Dijon-style mustard
- ❧ ½ cup chicken stock
- ❧ ½ cup fromage frais

- ❧ 1 tbsp. brandy (optional)
- ❧ salt and freshly ground black pepper

Garnish

- ❧ lemon slices
- ❧ fresh tarragon sprigs

Tarragon is a classic herb to accompany chicken. It has a powerful flavor and a tendency to turn bitter if cooked for too long, so care is required when using it.

1 Skin the chicken pieces and rub with the lemon juice.

2 Heat the oil in a pan and sauté the chicken pieces until well browned.

3 Add the remaining ingredients and pour on just enough cold water to half cover the chicken.

4 Cover with a tight fitting lid. Bring to a boil, then reduce to a simmer for 45 minutes or until the chicken is tender.

5 Remove chicken and keep warm while making the sauce.

6 Strain the cooking liquor into a measuring jug.

7 Heat the butter and the sunflower oil and sauté the garlic until softened. Stir in the tarragon and mustard and cook for a further minute.

8 Pour on the chicken stock and brandy, if used. Adjust seasoning to taste. Bring to a boil for 1 minute then reduce heat. Stir in the fromage frais.

9 Spoon the sauce over the served chicken pieces and garnish with a twist of lemon and fresh sprigs of tarragon.

Chicken Ardennaise

Serves 4

- 1½ lb. boneless chicken breast
- 2 thick center smoked ham slices, 4 oz. each
- 1 cup white wine
- 3 shallots or small sweet onions, finely chopped
- salt and freshly ground black pepper
- 2 tbsp. all-purpose flour
- 2 tbsp. butter
- 1 tbsp. vegetable oil
- ⅔ cup fromage frais
- 2 tsp. Dijon-style mustard
- 1 tbsp. chopped fresh parsley

This dish, good for special occasions, does need the attention of the cook at the last minute. Serve with rice or new potatoes and fresh garden vegetables.

1 Skin the chicken, and cut into bite-size pieces. Put in a bowl to one side.

2 Remove the rind and any fat from the ham and cut into julienne strips.

3 Place ham in a bowl, together with the white wine and onions. Mix well, cover, and leave to soak for 30 minutes. Drain, reserving the juice.

4 Lightly season the chicken, and turn in the flour until lightly dusted.

5 Heat together the butter and oil in a large skillet. Add the chicken and sauté for 4–5 minutes or until golden.

6 Add the ham and onions and cook for a further 2 minutes.

7 Pour on the reserved wine and fromage frais and simmer, gently, for a further 4–5 minutes.

8 Arrange chicken on a serving dish, cover and keep warm. Reduce the sauce a little over a high heat and stir in the mustard and parsley.

9 Spoon sauce over the chicken and serve immediately.

Dijon Chicken with Mushrooms

Serves 4

- 2 tbsp. olive oil
- 8 shallots or pickling onions, peeled
- seasoned flour
- 4 part-boned half chicken breasts, approx. 7 oz. each
- 1¼ cups chicken stock
- 1 tbsp. Dijon-style mustard
- 1 tsp. chopped fresh thyme
- 2 cups tiny button mushrooms, wiped
- salt and freshly ground black pepper

Garnish

- fresh thyme sprigs

Very quick to prepare for the unexpected guest. Although Dijon mustard is used in this recipe, try experimenting with wholegrain or one of the specialty mustards.

1 Heat the oil in a saucepan, add the shallots or onions and sauté until golden brown.

2 Skin the chicken breasts and dust lightly with the seasoned flour. Add to the pan and sauté until golden brown all over.

3 Add the chicken stock, mustard, thyme, and salt and pepper to taste. Cover and simmer for 15 minutes.

4 Add the mushrooms, and continue simmering, uncovered, for a further 15 minutes.

5 Serve immediately, garnished with sprigs of fresh thyme.

Coq au Vin

Serves 4

- 3½–4 lb. chicken
- 2 tbsp. vegetable oil
- 4 lean bacon slices, rinded and chopped
- 12 baby onions or shallots, peeled
- 2 cloves garlic, chopped
- 5 cups French red table wine
- 1 tbsp. brandy
- 1 tbsp. tomato paste
- 2 sprigs fresh thyme
- 2 bayleaves
- 2 sprigs fresh parsley
- 2½ cups small dark-gilled mushrooms
- salt and freshly ground black pepper
- 1 tbsp. all-purpose flour
- 1 tbsp. butter, softened

Garnish

- 2 tbsp. chopped fresh parsley

Originally the French farmer's simple stew using farmhouse chickens and wine from a neighboring vineyard, this dish is now a classic. As with many casseroles and stews, the flavor will improve if made a day or two in advance.

1 Joint the chicken into 8 portions.

2 Heat the oil in a large, heavy-based pan. Add the chicken in one single layer and sauté until evenly browned all over. Remove from the pan. Drain off all but 1 tbsp. fat from the pan.

3 Add the bacon, baby onions or shallots, and garlic to the pan and fry until the onions are golden. Stir in the red wine, brandy, tomato paste, fresh herbs, and seasoning, to taste.

4 Return the chicken to the pan. Bring to a boil, then reduce the heat, cover and simmer for 40 minutes. Stir in the mushrooms and simmer uncovered, for a further 10 minutes. Adjust seasoning, if necessary.

5 Transfer the chicken, onions, and mushrooms to a warm serving plate. Discard the herbs. Bring the sauce to a steady boil and drop in teaspoonfuls of the creamed flour and butter. Whisk continuously, until all the mixture has been added. Simmer for 10 minutes to cook the flour and thicken the sauce.

6 Pour the sauce over the chicken, then sprinkle with the freshly chopped parsley. Serve immediately, accompanied with fresh vegetables.

Almond and Sweet Pepper Chicken

Serves 4

- 4 boneless half chicken breasts, approx. 6 oz. each
- 6 tbsp. sunflower oil
- 1 medium onion, roughly chopped
- 1 inch fresh ginger, peeled
- 3 cloves garlic
- ¼ cup blanched almonds
- ¾ lb. sweet red bell peppers, seeded and chopped
- 1 tbsp. ground cumin
- 2 tsp. ground coriander
- 1 tsp. turmeric
- dash cayenne pepper
- ½ tsp. salt
- ⅔ cup water

- 3 whole star anise
- 2 tbsp. lemon juice
- freshly ground black pepper

A colorful chicken dish, enhanced with a nutty, spicy flavor that requires little accompaniment other than plain boiled rice.

1 Skin the chicken breasts and cut into pieces approximately 2 x ½ inch. Heat a third of the oil in a pan and cook the chicken for 5 minutes. Drain and transfer to a plate.

2 Combine the onion, ginger, garlic, almonds, sweet red peppers, cumin, coriander, turmeric, cayenne, and salt in a food processor or blender. Blend to a smooth paste.

3 Heat the remaining oil. Add the paste and cook for 10–12 minutes, stirring occasionally. Add the chicken pieces, water, star anise, lemon juice, and black pepper to taste. Cover, reduce the heat and simmer gently for 25 minutes or until the chicken is tender. Stir once or twice during cooking.

Chicken à la King

Serves 6

- 6 boneless half chicken breasts, approx. 5 oz. each
- 2 tbsp. butter
- 2 tbsp. vegetable oil
- 2½ cups button mushrooms, thickly sliced
- 1 sweet red bell pepper, seeded and cut into 1 inch squares
- 1 sweet yellow bell pepper, seeded and cut into 1 inch squares
- 1 sweet green bell pepper, seeded and cut into 1 inch squares
- few strands saffron, soaked in 2 tbsp. boiling water
- ⅔ cup chicken stock
- 1¼ cups fromage frais or low fat yogurt

- 2 tbsp. brandy or medium sherry
- 2 tsp. cornstarch
- salt and freshly ground black pepper

Garnish

- fresh watercress

This dish can be made a day or two in advance and kept covered in the refrigerator until required. Serve with plain boiled rice, to help mop up the juices.

1 Skin the chicken breasts and cut into bite-size pieces.

2 Heat the butter and half the oil in a large skillet. Add the mushrooms and sweet peppers and stir-fry until the peppers are just turning tender. Transfer, with a slotted spoon, onto paper towels, to drain.

3 Add the remaining oil to the pan and add the chicken pieces in a single layer. Sauté until golden brown. Season with salt and pepper.

4 Stir in the stock, fromage frais and the brandy and cornstarch, blended together. Continue to stir, over a low heat, until the sauce begins to thicken. Gently simmer, uncovered, for 5 minutes. Check seasoning and adjust if necessary.

5 Stir in the mushrooms and sweet peppers, and cook for a further 3–4 minutes. Serve on a bed of rice, garnished with fresh watercress.

Mediterranean Chicken with Feta and Green Olives

Serves 4

- ✤ 4 half chicken breasts
- ✤ flour, for dredging
- ✤ salt and freshly ground black pepper, to taste
- ✤ 6 tbsp. olive oil
- ✤ ¾ lb. button onions (or use large onions, quartered)
- ✤ 14 oz. can chopped tomatoes
- ✤ ½ cup boiling water
- ✤ 2 cups pitted green olives, washed and drained
- ✤ 1 tbsp. red wine vinegar
- ✤ 4 oz. feta cheese, sliced thinly

This dish originates from a region around Sparta. It is either prepared with olives or raisins, both being major products of this region.

1 Arrange the chicken breasts on a chopping board, dredge with the flour and season with salt and freshly ground black pepper on both sides.

2 Heat the oil in a large, deep skillet and add the chicken breasts, skin-side down. Cook on both sides for 3–5 minutes or until browned. Lift the chicken breasts out of the pan and set aside.

3 Add the onions to the skillet and sauté for about 5 minutes or until softened, stirring frequently. Return the chicken to the pan and add the chopped tomatoes and boiling water. Season with salt and freshly ground black pepper, cover, and simmer for 25–30 minutes or until the chicken is tender and cooked through, adding a little extra boiling water if necessary.

4 In the last 10 minutes of the cooking time, add the green olives and red wine vinegar. Stir to combine. Place a slice of feta cheese on top of each piece of chicken and continue to cook, uncovered, for a further 10 minutes, or until the cheese has just melted. Serve immediately.

Watercress Sauce on Chicken Breast

Serves 4

- 4 part-boned half chicken breasts, approx. 7 oz. each
- 2 oz. celery
- 2 oz. carrots, peeled
- 2 oz. string or snap beans, trimmed
- ⅔ cup chicken stock
- 1 bayleaf
- 2 tbsp. white wine
- 1 bunch watercress, trimmed of coarse stems
- 2 scallions, trimmed and chopped
- 6 tbsp. fromage frais
- 1 tsp. cornstarch, blended with 1 tsp. water
- salt and freshly ground black pepper

This chicken dish looks very fresh and colorful and provides sufficient vegetables to need only the addition of new potatoes when serving. If you have a steamer, cook the chicken over the stock for 25–30 minutes. The vegetables can also be steamed briefly.

1 Skin the chicken breasts and season lightly.

2 Prepare the vegetables and cut into julienne strips.

3 In a pan, bring the stock to a steady simmer. Add the chicken and bayleaf and cover with a tight fitting lid.

4 Cook gently for 35–40 minutes or until the chicken is tender.

5 Transfer the chicken to a warm serving plate. Add the seasoning and the scallions to the stock. (Remove the bayleaf.) Bring to a boil and rapidly bubble until it has reduced a little.

6 Add the white wine and the watercress, reserving a few leaves for the garnish. Remove the heat and allow to stand for one minute for the watercress to wilt.

7 Meanwhile, cook the vegetable julienne in boiling water until just *al dente* (cooked but firm when bitten) – no more than 5 minutes. Drain and keep warm.

8 Strain the stock into a measuring jug. Transfer the watercress and scallions to a food processor or blender and add 6 tbsp. stock, the fromage frais and the blended cornstarch. Purée to a smooth sauce. Season to taste.

9 Reheat gently, stirring, until thickened. Adjust the consistency of the sauce with a little more stock if desired.

10 To serve, place each chicken breast on a plate. Spoon over the vegetables julienne and pour the watercress sauce around the chicken. Garnish with the reserved watercress leaves.

Ricotta and Chicken with Fresh Tomato and Basil Sauce

Serves 6

- 🍃 6 boneless half chicken breasts, skinned, approx. 6 oz. each
- 🍃 1 lb. fresh spinach
- 🍃 6 oz. ricotta cheese
- 🍃 ½ cup pinenuts
- 🍃 salt and freshly ground black pepper
- 🍃 1¼ cups chicken stock

Sauce

- 🍃 1 lb. fresh tomatoes, skinned
- 🍃 1 tbsp. sunflower oil
- 🍃 1 small onion, diced
- 🍃 1 tbsp. tomato paste
- 🍃 1 tsp. superfine sugar
- 🍃 salt and freshly ground black pepper
- 🍃 2 tbsp. chopped fresh basil

Garnish

- 🍃 fresh basil leaves

A very pretty dish, fresh with the vibrant colors of the tomato sauce and spinach filling. Accompany with a salad and new potatoes.

1 Flatten each chicken breast, in turn, by beating between 2 pieces of damp wax paper with a rolling pin.

2 Remove the spinach leaves from the main stem and wash well. Shake well, put in a large dry pan and cook until wilted and reduced in volume. Drain, squeezing well to remove excess liquid. Chop finely.

3 Mix together the spinach, ricotta, pinenuts, and seasoning. Divide the filling between the breasts and spread over each, leaving ½ inch gap on one long edge. Roll up each roulade starting with the opposite edge, and secure loosely with strong cotton or fine string. Wrap each breast in a piece of foil and lay in an ovenproof dish.

4 Pour in the stock and poach gently at 400°F for 30 minutes, or until the chicken is cooked through.

5 Meanwhile make the sauce. Chop the tomatoes roughly. Heat the oil and cook gently until softened. Add the tomatoes, paste, sugar and seasoning. Simmer for 30 minutes.

6 Blend until smooth. Check the seasoning, then stir in the chopped basil. Keep warm until required, then divide between 6 warm plates.

7 To serve, remove the chicken, each breast cut into neat slices and arrange on top of the sauce on each plate. Garnish with fresh basil leaves.

Piquant Chicken

Serves 4

- 8 chicken thighs
- 2 tbsp. sunflower oil
- 5 whole cloves garlic, unpeeled
- 5 tbsp. red wine vinegar
- 1¼ cups dry white wine
- 2 tbsp. brandy
- 2 tsp. Dijon-style mustard
- 2 tsp. tomato paste
- ⅔ cup low fat fromage frais
- 2 tomatoes, skinned and seeded and cut into thin strips
- salt and freshly ground black pepper

The lively, piquant flavor of this sharp sauce transforms these economical chicken thighs into a special treat. Accompany with some plain boiled new potatoes and sweet early season peas.

1 Heat the oil in a large heavy-based saucepan. Cook the chicken thighs, turning, until evenly browned. Add the garlic cloves, and reduce the heat. Cover and simmer for 20 minutes or until the chicken is tender.

2 Drain all but 1 tbsp. fat from the pan. Add the vinegar and stir well, scraping up any sediment from the bottom. Boil rapidly until the liquid is reduced to approximately 2 tbsp. Transfer the chicken to a serving dish and keep warm.

3 Add the wine, brandy, mustard, and tomato paste to the pan, stir well and rapidly boil until reduced to a thick sauce (approximately 5 minutes).

4 In another small saucepan, heat the fromage frais until warmed through. Place a sieve over the saucepan, and pour on the vinegar sauce, pressing the garlic cloves well to remove the pulp. Remove sieve. Season to taste.

5 Stir the tomatoes into the sauce. Reheat if necessary and pour over the chicken to serve.

Filbert Chicken Normandy

Serves 4

- 4 boneless half chicken breasts, approx. 5 oz. each skinned
- 1 tbsp. seasoned all-purpose flour
- 2 tbsp. butter
- 1 tbsp. light olive oil
- 4 tbsp. Applejack (optional)
- 1¼ cups medium cider
- ⅔ cup fromage frais or light cream
- 2 tbsp. filberts, coarsely chopped

Garnish

- 2 eating apples
- 1 tbsp. lemon juice
- 1 tbsp. butter

This is definitely a recipe for that special occasion. The delicious combination of chicken in a creamy cider sauce, apples and filberts needs only fresh garden vegetables to set it off.

1 Split the chicken breasts, but not all the way through, and open out and flatten to form a neat butterfly shape. Dust with the flour.

2 Heat the butter and oil in a pan and brown the breasts on each side. If using the Applejack heat it in a small pan or ladle, ignite with a match and pour, flaming, onto the chicken. Pour in the cider, cover and simmer until the breasts are tender and cooked. Remove and keep warm.

3 While the chicken is simmering, cut the unpeeled apples into wedges or thick slices. Remove the cores and toss in lemon juice. Sauté the apple in the butter until heated through but still firm.

4 Boil the cooking liquid to reduce by half. Taste and adjust seasoning. Stir in fromage frais or cream and filberts. Gently reheat.

5 Serve each chicken breast with some sauce spooned over it and the remainder passed round separately. Garnish with the apple wedges or slices. Serve immediately.

Lemon Chicken Greek-style

Serves 6-8

- 3½ lb. chicken, without giblets, cut into small portions
- ¼ cup butter
- salt and freshly ground black pepper, to taste
- 1¼ cups boiling water
- 1 bunch scallions, trimmed and cut into 1 inch pieces
- 3 eggs
- 3 tbsp. freshly squeezed lemon juice

Garnish

- 2 tbsp. chopped fresh dill

Chicken flavored with lemon is such a delicious combination of tastes and one that is commonly found in Greece. There is plenty of sauce in this dish so rice would be a welcome accompaniment.

1 Melt the butter in a large, heavy-based saucepan and add the chicken. Cook for about 5 minutes, or until evenly browned, turning and rearranging during cooking.

2 Season the chicken with salt and freshly ground black pepper, and add the boiling water and the scallions. Cover and simmer for 35–40 minutes, or until the chicken is tender and cooked through.

3 Place the eggs in a small bowl and beat well. Gradually whisk in the lemon juice, a little at a time to prevent curdling. Whisk in 1¼ cups of the cooking liquid from the chicken. Pour the egg and lemon mixture over the chicken and stir continuously until the sauce has thickened slightly. Do not boil.

4 Transfer the chicken and sauce to a warm serving dish and sprinkle with the chopped fresh dill.

Honey Rum Chicken with Mushroom Sauce

Serves 4

- *4 large half chicken breasts, boned, skinned and fat cut off*
- *¼ cup orange juice*
- *1 tbsp. honey*
- *1½ tbsp. clarified butter*
- *2 cloves garlic, minced*
- *1 cup button mushrooms, sliced*
- *1 cup oyster mushrooms, sliced*
- *1 cup dark rum*
- *2 cups chicken stock*
- *salt and freshly ground black pepper*
- *½ cup light cream*
- *2 eggs, beaten*
- *2 tbsp. chopped fresh cilantro*

Garnish

- *orange slices (optional)*

Serve the sauce over the chicken and accompany with cooked vegetables, pasta or rice.

1 Poke several holes in the chicken breasts with a knife point. Mix the orange juice and honey and marinate the chicken in it for 20 minutes. In a large, heavy-based skillet, brown the chicken in 1 tbsp. clarified butter. Remove from the heat and set aside.

2 Melt the remaining butter in the same skillet, then add the garlic and mushrooms and fry for 1 minute. Pour in the rum and flame it.

3 Add the chicken stock, salt and pepper and chicken and simmer over a low heat for 30 minutes.

4 Just before serving, beat the cream with the eggs and add to the skillet. Cook over low heat for about 1 minute.

5 Add the cilantro, check the seasoning and cook for a further 1 minute.

6 Garnish with orange slices, if desired, and serve

Vinegar Sauce and Chicken Casserole

Serves 8

- 🐾 2 x 3 lb. chickens
- 🐾 7 cloves garlic
- 🐾 3 large tomatoes
- 🐾 1 tsp. peppercorns
- 🐾 1 cup red wine vinegar
- 🐾 scant 2 cups chicken stock
- 🐾 salt and freshly ground black pepper
- 🐾 7 oz. fromage frais

Garnish

- 🐾 3 tbsp. chopped chives

This is the perfect dish for a large party, as it is economical, can be made in advance and reheated, and has an enticing sweet-sour aroma. Accompany the dish with fresh noodles or soft creamed potatoes.

1 Divide each chicken into 8 portions, diagonally halving the breasts. Carefully remove the bones.

2 Peel and mince the garlic. Skin, seed and roughly chop the tomatoes.

3 Heat a large non-stick skillet; there is no need for any oil. In batches, brown the chicken portions on all sides for 6 minutes. Remove the chicken pieces and leave to cool on a wire rack.

4 Transfer the chicken to a large casserole. Add garlic, tomatoes, and peppercorns and cook for 1 minute.

5 Add the vinegar and boil for 3–4 minutes to reduce the liquid. Heat the stock, cover and simmer for 10 minutes until the chicken is tender.

6 Remove the chicken from the casserole and allow the pieces to cool again on the wire rack.

Chicken Véronique

Serves 4

- 🐾 4 boneless half chicken breasts, approx. 6 oz. each, skinned
- 🐾 1 cup chicken stock
- 🐾 4 tbsp. dry white wine
- 🐾 rind and juice ½ lemon
- 🐾 2 tsp. finely chopped onion
- 🐾 1 bayleaf
- 🐾 sprig tarragon (or dash dried)
- 🐾 3 peppercorns
- 🐾 2 tsp. cornstarch
- 🐾 4 tbsp. fromage frais
- 🐾 salt and white pepper

Garnish

- 🐾 fresh tarragon (optional)

Véronique describes the smooth white wine sauce and sweet grapes that contribute to this classic dish. Chicken, ham and sole can be prepared this way. This recipe has been adapted to maintain sophistication, but lower the calories.

Stovetop Creamy Chicken

7 Bring the liquid in the casserole to a boil again and simmer it gently until it is the consistency of light cream. Skim off any fatty froth from time to time.

8 When there is approximately 2½ cups sauce, strain through a fine sieve. Season to taste with pepper and, if required some salt.

9 Return the chicken pieces and the sauce to the casserole. The sauce should half cover the chicken.

10 Gently reheat the casserole. Swirl in the fromage frais and sprinkle with the freshly chopped chives. Serve hot.

1 Place the stock, white wine, lemon rind, onion, tarragon, bayleaf, and peppercorns in a saucepan. Bring to a boil then reduce the heat and simmer. Lightly season the chicken breasts and poach them in liquid for 20 minutes or until tender. (The pan must be covered with a lid.)

2 Meanwhile, peel and pit the grapes and toss in the lemon. Leave to stand.

3 Transfer the cooked chicken to a serving dish and keep warm. Heat the stock and return to the saucepan. Boil until reduced by half.

4 Blend the cornstarch with a little cold water (or wine) and stir into saucepan; continue to boil, stirring, until smooth and thickened. Season to taste.

5 Remove from the heat and stir in the drained grapes and the fromage frais. Pour the sauce over the chicken and serve immediately, garnish if you like, with a sprig of fresh tarragon.

Serves 4

- ❦ 2 tbsp. vegetable oil
- ❦ 2 tbsp. butter or margarine
- ❦ 4 skinned boneless half chicken breasts, trimmed of fat
- ❦ 1½ cups chicken stock; or use bouillon cubes
- ❦ 1 tsp. crumbled thyme leaves
- ❦ 1 cup sour cream, or reduced-fat sour cream
- ❦ ½ tsp. cornstarch
- ❦ 5 oz. No-cook Mojito (page 121)

This has a rich, creamy taste but need not wreck your diet if you use reduced-fat sour cream rather than the heavy-duty stuff.

1 In a large skillet over medium heat, heat the oil and butter. Add the chicken and sauté until golden, about 2 minutes on each side. Add stock and thyme and bring to a boil.

2 Lower heat, cover and simmer for 15 minutes or until the chicken is cooked through and juices run clear. Remove chicken to warm platter.

3 In a small bowl, stir together sour cream and cornstarch. Stir in No-cook Mojito until blended.

4 Stir the mixture into juice in pan. Simmer for 2 minutes, stirring occasionally, until slightly thickened.

5 Pour the sauce over the chicken and serve immediately.

Poached Chicken with Melon

Serves 4

- 🍃 1½ cups chicken stock
- 🍃 4 skinned, boneless half chicken breasts, trimmed of fat
- 🍃 3 tbsp. red wine vinegar
- 🍃 1 tbsp. firmly packed dark brown sugar
- 🍃 2 cloves garlic, minced
- 🍃 1 tsp. minced fresh ginger root
- 🍃 1 tsp. Dijon-style mustard
- 🍃 ¾ cup diced mango
- 🍃 ½ cup orange-flesh melon balls
- 🍃 ½ cup cantaloupe balls

Garnish
- 🍃 freshly snipped chives (optional)

This unusual and refreshing chilled dish looks 5-star restaurant pretty when served with wild rice. Instead of a tossed salad, try chilled asparagus drizzled with vinaigrette. You might want to serve this on chilled plates. Glass or crystal plates are perfect.

1 In a medium-sized skillet, bring the stock to a boil, then reduce heat to low and simmer. Add the chicken, cover and simmer, until cooked through and the juices run clear — about 10 minutes.

2 With a slotted spatula, remove the chicken from the skillet. Leave to cool, then cover and refrigerate until chilled — about 2 hours.

3 Meanwhile, boil stock until reduced to ½ cup. Stir in remaining ingredients, except melon balls, and cook, stirring frequently for 5 minutes.

4 Gently stir in melon balls and diced mango. Toss to coat.

5 Refrigerate until chilled for about 2 hours.

6 Garnish with snipped chives and serve.

Index